Footpath to Freedom

By Linda McBurney-Gunhouse

Published by:
Creative Focus Publishing
Winnipeg Beach, Manitoba
Canada

Cover photo & artwork by Linda McBurney-Gunhouse
ISBN: 978-1-928071-26-6

Copyright © 2007 Linda McBurney-Gunhouse
Revised 2025
All Rights Reserved.
R.5

Published by:
Creative Focus Publishing
Winnipeg Beach, Manitoba R0C 3G0 Canada
info@creativefocus.ca

Please visit our website:
www.creativefocus.ca

All Scripture is taken from the King James Version of the Bible unless otherwise stated.

A Note from the Author

Footpath to Freedom is about steps we can take that will lead us into a freedom that will touch every area of our lives. The freedom we explore in this book is freedom from many emotional, mental, physical, and spiritual things we struggle with every single day. Written from a spiritual perspective, it refers to many Biblical verses that all have to do with the freedom a true faith in Jesus Christ brings.

You may think that finding true freedom is fiction, and not a reality, but I am happy to say that after struggling for many years to find true freedom, I found it. If you are tired of feeling there's no escape and can find no way out of your predicaments, I believe you will benefit from this book, especially as you apply the many ideas offered.

My prayer for you is that as you begin on this footpath to freedom, that with each step you courageously take, you will discover that you have a Friend who infinitely loves you and has made a way for you to enjoy a freedom unsurpassed by any other. I pray also that you will find the joy and fulfillment in your life that this new freedom will offer. God bless you as you begin on this path.

In His service,
Linda McBurney-Gunhouse
Winnipeg Beach, MB

This book is dedicated to the many people who have contributed in some way to the many avenues of freedom I enjoy today. Mostly, I give thanks and praise to Jesus, who opened wide my prison doors and set me free to be all I am and all I continue to reach out to be.

Contents

Introduction 1
Chapter 1 — True Freedom 3
   Are We Really Free? 3
   A Slave to Addiction 4
   The Path to Freedom 5
   A Hidden Enemy & His Greatest Tool 6
   Superficial Happiness 9
Chapter 2 — Handling Emotional Ups & Downs . 11
   Physical Changes 11
   Aging & Relocation 12
   Celebrations & Seasons 13
   Hidden Emotional Issues 13
   The Problem of Anger 14
   Pride & Envy 16
   The Best Friend Ever 17
Chapter 3 — A Clean House 19
   Coming Clean 19
   Beware of Control 21
   Cleaning House 23
   Covering with Prayer 24
Chapter 4 — People Problems 27
   Ways We Communicate 27
   The Right Way to Communicate 29
   Learning Good Communication Skills 30
   The Enemy of Guilt 32
   When Worry Assails Us 33
   Healthy Relationships 34
Chapter 5 — The Problem With Self 37
   Discerning Who We Are 38
   Prideful Self 39
   Judging & Being Judged 40
   The Problem with Self-Esteem 41

How Self Traps Us..42
Taking on Others' Problems..................................43
How to Be Free..44

Chapter 6 — From Hardships to Plenty..........47
An Open Door..48
Closed Doors..49
A Turn-Around...51
God at Work...52
A Miracle Unfolds..53
God Fulfills My Dreams..54

Chapter 7 — Strategic Thinking....................57
Words of Encouragement......................................58
Beware of the Source...59
Fear vs. Faith Thoughts...60
Submitting to God...61
The Right Focus..62
A Clear Focus..63
Thoughts & Obedience..65

Chapter 8 — Exploring New Territory............67
1. Rid Our Minds of Fear..67
   Finding Enjoyment..69
   Beware of the Enemy.......................................71
2. Become Proactive Against Fear......................71
   Be Prepared for Battle.....................................72
3. Explore New Thoughts & Ideas.......................74

Chapter 9 — Balancing Act 77
The Importance of Prioritizing..............................78
Beware of Over-extending Yourself.....................79
Life-Change Stress...80
The Bane of Busyness...82
Benefits of Fellowship..84
Waiting on the Lord..85

Chapter 10 — Dare to Dream..................87
    Word Pictures.. 89
    The Right Dreams... 90
    A Dream Come True 92
    Sharing Your Giftings 93
    A Fresh Vision... 94

The Way of Salvation..............................97
About the Author 101
Other Titles.. 103

Introduction

We live in a world of endless possibilities, yet sometimes we feel as if the world is closing in around us. We may start out free, but through the course of many events and commitments, we find ourselves in over our heads, and then we wonder how we can ever get back to a simpler, happier time in our lives. Many things can make us feel trapped, and we wonder how to escape from it all. We might be struggling in our jobs or with difficult people in our lives. We may be limited by financial resources or find ourselves suddenly unemployed. What do we do with the many demands placed on us and yet experience a freedom in it all? We may plan trips, join health clubs, and even drop out of some commitments, yet we keep finding ourselves back in our own little prisons of life, unable to free ourselves.

Footpath to Freedom offers hope and answers for the freedom we all seek and long for. You may think it means a drive in the country or a flight away to some exotic island. But freedom is not necessarily escaping from the day to day. Rather, it is embracing all of life without becoming so entangled in it that we feel we are suffocating. Although it may not seem so, freedom is never far away. It is as close as a prayer and the faith we have to believe in the One who will set us free, and then set us on a path, a footpath where we continue to learn to walk in that freedom, trusting Him along the way.

As well as faith, we discover in this book that freedom has a lot to do with our thoughts. All my life, I struggled with my thoughts, and I wondered, "What makes a person happy?" and "How can I learn to control my thoughts, so that I am both peaceful and relatively happy?" Suffering with the blues or depression, I also felt an intense feeling of "no escape." I wondered, where does true freedom lie, and how can I live a life free of and in spite of the many cares that I must deal with every day? What resulted is many years of reading, researching and searching for answers. But the best insights have come from my own struggles and personal experiences, which I share throughout the book.

I invite you to explore with me this fascinating and somewhat elusive topic of freedom. As you read, I pray that you will experience a new freedom, which will result in a much more joyful and fruitful life for you.

And I will walk at liberty: for I seek thy precepts.
Psalm 119:45

Chapter 1
True Freedom

Have you ever had a big, emotional experience that you'll never forget? You were so happy, you were on cloud nine and thought you'd never come down from it? I'm not talking about a temporary drug high or even the high you get from endorphins when you exercise, like jogging or cycling. I'm not talking about graduating or getting a job promotion, traveling, or anything like that. I'm talking about an EXPERIENCE that changed your life forever in a good way. I wonder how many people have these kinds of life-changing experiences? I've heard parents say they felt that high when they first held their newborn baby. Some couples feel this when they first get married, and especially if they have been chaste (no sex before marriage). The title of this chapter is about freedom, and it's that kind of life-changing experience I'm going to talk about, the kind that sets you free.

Are We Really Free?

Did you know that the source of your pain, depression and anxiety has to do with how free you are right now? Think about that for a moment. Many times, we don't realize that we're not really free. We might live in a "free" country and have all kinds of freedoms that those living under oppressive regimes don't have. Some people aren't free to work where they want, worship where they please and who they please, are not free to marry a person of their choice, and so on. Years ago, there were lords, also called masters, and they had slaves. The Children of Israel, around the time of Moses, were slaves to the Egyptians, who treated them cruelly and had no mercy on them. Truly, a slave was not free and recognized their bondage to their cruel masters. So what do I mean when I say we may not be free, when we live in a free country and are not a slave to any demanding master?

I'd like to answer that with a personal story. When I was about 18, I was suffering with the full effects of a nervous breakdown. I had hit bottom from all the drugs I had done and the ungodly life I was living. I had moved away from home and was lonely, had no boundaries, got into a cult, and hung out with the wrong crowd from college. A romantic relationship had failed, and everything caught up with me. I ended up going to a full gospel Bible School in Saskatchewan, thanks to the support of my parents and my uncle. It was here that I was introduced to Jesus, the Healer of all broken hearts and sick bodies, bruised emotions and mixed-up minds. It was here that, for the first time ever, I recognized that I was not truly free. In fact, it wasn't until AFTER the Lord Jesus touched my heart and life and made all things new, that I looked back at the horror of my life and realized how much a slave I was to the life I had been living.

A Slave to Addiction

If you have ever been addicted to something, then you know you are a slave to that habit, whatever it might be (alcohol, drugs, gambling, sex, etc.). I was addicted to drugs. I couldn't go for one day without getting high, because it was the only time I wasn't sad and depressed. But the high was very short-lived, and of course, I had to keep up with the habit in order to continue to get the high. Then, after I got supernaturally freed from this addiction, other addictions cropped up. I was once told through a very wise and godly counselor, that I was addicted to people. I had to have the comfort of people around me at all times, and I couldn't go without being in a relationship, especially with boyfriends. I was also supernaturally freed from this addiction. For each addiction, I had to be delivered supernaturally by prayer. This is no big thing to do, although the addiction seems overpowering. Praying is easy, and it's nothing for God to deliver us in an instant. Sometimes it takes a little longer, depending on what God wants to do in your life. The main thing is to hand it over to Him and then do what He tells you to do if it is not instantly taken from you. There is no magic formula to prayer — all you need to do is believe and receive.

The Path to Freedom

About the same time the Lord took away my desire and need to do drugs, He also took away my intense like and addiction to the ungodly rock music I was listening to. The two went hand-in-hand, the drugs and the rock and roll music. He gave me alternative contemporary Christian music that soothed me and helped speed the healing of my emotions and physical ailments. It seemed that as one by one He took away the things that were harmful to me and that I was addicted to, that my emotions and thoughts changed dramatically. I was also on a routine schedule as a student of the Bible School, and I was eating properly for a diabetic diet (no sugar or white breads). I was getting proper sleep and exercise. I was feeding my mind the nutritious food of the Word of God, and His Word was changing my thoughts, my heart, and my very life. In fact, I remember one day I felt so good I didn't know what to do with myself.

But there was more to come. The Lord realized that I needed a rite of passage; I needed to know beyond a shadow of a doubt that I was truly free, so He allowed me to experience the full effects of being set free! One night, with the full audience and support of the student body, staff and ministers at the church at the Bible School, the Lord touched my life and literally took away all my sins and with it my regretful past that had been weighing me down for so many years. I felt the heaviness in my heart lift. I don't know how He does this, but He cleaned up my heart and then made me a new creature in Christ. I knew I was born again and His child. I realized that all of the old rotten life I had been a slave to was gone and, truly, I was free. It was much more than a feeling — I knew with every fibre of my being that I was truly free. This is something to celebrate! I let everyone know, and to this day, I celebrate that life-changing experience by sharing my story with others, in hopes that they will reach out to Jesus and receive their own life-changing experience of freedom. Now who wouldn't want that? But if you don't know you are a slave, you will not see a need for freedom.

A Hidden Enemy & His Greatest Tool

But is everything perfect after we have such an incredible mountain-top experience? No, for trials begin almost immediately since we need to grow in our new-found faith. It took me many years to uncover what lay at the heart of my depression and sadness, which would appear time and again throughout my life. I have had to learn and re-learn that the only thing that makes me a slave and tries to keep me a slave is sin and the devil, who initiated the act of sinning against God in the first place. The first insight I am offering you as a way to freedom in your thinking and in your life is to reveal the source of all that is negative and restricting in our lives, whether we are professing Christians or not. <u>At the heart of all sadness and sorrow is SIN and the devil, who will try everything in his power to keep you a slave to it. As long as you are not free, then you are a slave to sin in some form. The devil, who is the author of everything evil and negative in your life, has deceived you by your own permission or because you have rejected Jesus Christ, or neglected His Word, which is the Truth.</u>

That's a pretty big pill to swallow, and I want you to re-read the underlined words again. Remember in the Book of Genesis when the serpent tempted Eve and caused her to question God's Word? (see Genesis 3). The serpent mesmerized Eve with a poison lie that caused her to sin and then doomed us, since through her womb, we would all be born slaves to sin. Satan's game plan was to seize control of our soul (mind, emotions and will), so that God would lose, so he cleverly tempted us with a knowledge that didn't come from God. Like Eve, who was temporarily dazed into obeying Satan's suggestion, we too walk around in a daze, unhappy and depressed, not even realizing that we've been duped by the greatest deceiver that ever walked this earth. We become slaves to negative thinking and become trapped in a maze of poisonous lies, thinking there is no escape and that our situation is hopeless.

God promised Adam and Eve that a Deliverer would come and set us free from the power of sin and loose us from the control and usurped powers of wicked Satan. Two thousand years later, Jesus Christ, God's own Son, came and lived on this earth and then died for all our sins, past, present and future. He set us free from the power of sin so we would no longer be slaves to it any longer. We can't hope to know true freedom without first acquainting ourselves with the Lord, the only One who can truly set us free from sin, sickness, addictions, and anything that causes us pain or duress.

What Jesus, our Messiah, did is described in the following:

> *The Spirit of the Lord GOD is upon me; because the LORD hath anointed me to preach good tidings unto the meek; he hath sent me to bind up the brokenhearted, to proclaim liberty to the captives, <u>and the opening of the prison to them that are bound</u>; Isaiah 61:1*

Notice the last part that is underlined. Only Jesus could, can and will open the prison doors **to them that are bound**, and that includes each and every one of us.

In the New Testament, the following verse describes in a nutshell what happened and what happens when we reach for any other freedom than what Jesus Christ offers:

> *While they promise them liberty, they themselves are the servants of corruption: for of whom a man is overcome, of the same is he brought in bondage. 2 Peter 2:19*

Chapter 1 - True Freedom

In this verse, we can again picture a slave/master relationship. Anything that overcomes us will become our master, and we will be a slave to it. Sin does that. We become slaves to sin and live under its tyranny. Only Jesus can free us from sin.

Superficial Happiness

Do you see that there is a definite connection regarding sin and freedom from sin to how we think, whether positive or negative? You may be a Christian and are thinking, **What about my non-Christian friends who seem to be positive and happy? If they are slaves to sin, why aren't they depressed or sad?** The Bible says that the pleasure of sin is only for a season (see Hebrews 11:25). Also, without a knowledge of our sin, we can think we are happy and free, but the Bible is very clear about this — **the wages of sin is death** (see Romans 6:23). So even though our non-Christian friends seem to be enjoying their life now, unless they come to terms with their sin, sadly, they will spend eternity without God. We need to pray for them that they see their need of a Savior before it's too late for them.

We are born with the desire to be free. Before we come to Jesus and start our life over, we search for peace and happiness. We may strive to have lots of money so we can buy anything we want, travel the world over, or surround ourselves with people and go to every party going. Yet, still, we come home to an empty feeling. Freedom and happiness elude us, so we go from one thrill or pleasure to the next. We see Hollywood movie stars and famous people living empty lives, going from one partner to the next, or hiding in their multi-million-dollar homes, afraid to be seen in public. We think of Princess Diana, hounded by the paparazzi, contributing to her early death. Even the rich and famous live in their own form of prisons, perhaps much worse than any of us would ever know. So we know that fame and fortune do not give us the happiness we all need and seek. True freedom from our sin will give us a peaceful heart and a mind free of the clutter and cares of the world. We will feel the comfort of the Holy Spirit with us, no matter what happens or what kind of day we are having. Nothing in this world can give us what only Jesus can give us. If you don't know Jesus personally, the One true freedom-giver, please turn to "The Way of Salvation" near the end of the book, and follow the prayer guide offered, so that by faith in Him, you can begin your journey of freedom today.

In the next chapter, we're going to discuss life's ups and downs and explore ideas on how to arrive at a more even keel, so that we can maintain a positive attitude no matter what.

Chapter 2
Handling Emotional Ups & Downs

Once we are freed from a lifetime of slavery to sin, and we know we are free through Jesus, we will soon discover that life is not all a bed of roses. So then what? Life will assail us with troubles, struggles and trials. This is a guarantee. Some people will seem to come through unscathed, like Job, and continue praising the Lord. Some will not. Some of us struggle with on-going emotional problems, just as others struggle with ongoing physical problems like arthritis or allergies. So we want to look at some possible causes of emotional ups and downs.

Physical Changes

Sometimes physical problems cause emotional upsets. Women, for instance, suffer with hormonal issues. Emotional swings will be normal throughout most of her life. Boyfriends and husbands soon discover to beware and keep a distance at "that time of the month." Tempers might flare, and a general grouchiness fills the air as women suffer with over-tiredness, cramps, and a feeling of the blues. Every woman appreciates an understanding man, especially at this time of the month. Then there are children going into adolescence who experience hormonal changes. As a high school teacher, we are trained in how to teach these children going into junior high. They can be the most mischievous, boisterous and fun group to teach. They are still children, but have the maturity and desire to reach for more adult responsibilities. It is at this crucial stage in their life that they need the most guidance, patience, and understanding, not to mention discipline.

As mentioned in the Introduction, this is the age when I began to experience depression for the first time ever. So this is an age group that should never be overlooked for the beginnings of depression or other behavioral and emotional problems. This is also the age many of them will start to experiment with drugs, alcohol and even sex. With the right counseling, adolescents can be and need to be reached early enough to stave off a lifetime of further problems.

Aging & Relocation

Another vulnerable age group for emotional ups and downs is seniors, especially those who lose their home and familiar way of life and are forced to move into an apartment or even a nursing home. The lifestyle change is so dramatic that an emotional toll on their health is sometimes inevitable, at least temporarily. Yet, I have seen very well-adjusted residents living in nursing homes. I had a cousin who was 103, living in a nursing home. She accepted her lot many years earlier when she could no longer care for herself. We never heard her complain about living in the nursing home. Yet others chronically complain and are not happy there, no matter how well they are treated, fed, or how nice their surroundings are. Still, we should not neglect people who are in nursing homes, even if all we do is pray for their comfort and happiness. Some churches offer services complete with singing and a sermon to provide spiritual nourishment, and then they enjoy food and fellowship afterwards.

Celebrations & Seasons

Other times, there are circumstantial events that trigger emotional ups and downs. Adults and children of all ages experience natural highs and lows, especially at around holiday time. Take Christmas, for instance. We spend weeks preparing for Christmas: planning for special concerts, shopping for gifts, caroling, writing greeting cards, planning a delicious menu, decorating, and visiting friends and relatives. It's truly a wonderful time of year, and even a good snowfall adds to the ambience of the "good" feelings in the air. Downtowns are glittering with Christmas lights, and we enjoy driving up and down the streets looking at all the beautifully decorated yards and houses.

Then, after New Years, we might bask in the memories of the season for awhile, still enjoying our memories of the joyous season and lovingly putting away our gifts. Then, when all the decorations are finally put away, a feeling of deflation hits us, and we have what we call the "January blues." Or after summer holidays, especially if we have really enjoyed the summer, we settle into our routines once again, and it seems like the party's over. Fall sets in, and the days become shorter. We go back to work (whether out or at home), where we are forced to stay inside, and the kids go back to a busy schedule in school.

Hidden Emotional Issues

Then, there are other emotional highs and lows that seem to constantly persist, regardless of physical problems and natural occurrences that happen throughout life. When I was in my late 20s, I came to recognize that I had a problem with my emotional life and no matter what

I tried, nothing seemed to work. I was down more than I was up, and the answer to leading a normal life eluded me. I was very fortunate to receive professional help from a trained psychiatrist who knew what to do. He suggested I attend a self-help group. I remember the first time I attended such a group. I was nervous, because this was an open group and I didn't know anybody there. I had to share something about myself, as everyone else did that night. But when my turn came to speak, I simply shared how I was feeling. That night, I made a major discovery about myself — I had a problem with anger. Every time I attended this meeting, I must have sounded like a stuck record — anger was the feeling I was struggling with each time I shared, and it was anger that was at the core of my emotional problems. Later, I discovered that anger unexpressed or not expressed in a healthy way, leads to depression.

The Problem of Anger

In fact, I also learned that anger is at the heart of the problem for many drug addicts and alcoholics, only they don't know this until they seek help or join a group that deals with these addictions, like I did. Negative behavior and the harmful and destructive emotions that accompany it have to start somewhere, and sometimes we become so entrenched in the addiction or negative thought patterns we are in that we wouldn't even know where to begin to trace its roots. We learned in the first chapter that sin is responsible for all that is negative in our lives, yet throughout our lifetime, we will struggle with sin in one form or another. This is why we need to be vigilant in going to the only One who knows us inside and out. Jesus will

Chapter 2 - Handling Emotional Ups & Downs

reveal what is in our hearts that is causing us to stumble, or the thing that is holding us captive and preventing us from enjoying the freedom we're entitled to. In my case, He led me to this wonderful self-help group.

I remember sharing with the group that I was angry at other drivers who would cut me off or steal a parking space I wanted. I was angry with my boss for the way he treated me at work, showing little or no respect. And through the years, wherever there were people congregating, like jobs, churches, groups, clubs or whatever, there always seemed to be cliques who would only include certain ones into their inner circle of friends. If I felt left out, I felt angry that people would treat me so poorly. I felt angry that I always had to work hard for every success in life, even though others seemed to have things handed to them on a silver platter. Their success was effortless, while mine was an uphill battle. I felt like I always had to prove something, that I wasn't quite good enough the way that I was. So I felt angry that I had to work harder at everything, including my education, my appearance, and my overall attitude.

It was truly enlightening to uncover this much anger that I was carrying around with me, and that I had felt this way for so long! No wonder I wasn't happy. How could I be, since anger is all-consuming and will steal whatever joy we may have? Something miraculous would have to happen in my heart and life to cause me to give up my anger and be able to accept myself, and celebrate who I am, differences and all. Many of the answers I needed came to me while attending this self-help group. By opening up and sharing, reading pertinent literature, praying, and engaging in personal soul-searching, I began to find healing.

Pride & Envy

One of the most important things I learned is that anger has another deep root, and it's called self-centered pride. It really begins with pride. If you go back to the Book of Genesis, Cain killed Abel out of self-centered pride. He couldn't be happy for his brother, that God accepted Abel's sacrifice, and not his. So, out of an uncontrolled rage and anger, he slew his own brother. If you think about it, any time we do not get our own way, or we feel that someone else is getting more and better than us, anger and self-centered pride will rear up, and we won't be able to see clearly enough to love that person who has stolen a limelight we think we should have had. It happens in families all the time when one sibling gets more attention than the other. It happens in the workplace when a co-worker gets the promotion we think we should have had. It happens when someone is suddenly blessed financially, and yet we still continue to struggle just to pay our monthly bills. It happens at some point in a thousand ways to each and every one of us. It is no wonder we are sad, depressed and discontent when there will always be someone or something we can compare our own lives to and feel we have been cheated in some way.

In my situation, the Lord had begun a tremendous healing work in my heart when I was still in Bible School. This enabled me to get through many years, before I came to an almost complete standstill again, seeking a self-help group for answers. The Bible School was situated in the middle of the Saskatchewan prairies. I used to love walking by myself up and down the sloping hills with golden wheat fields on both sides of the gravel road and no trees to block the magnificent view of the prairie skies. Here it was quiet and peaceful, with nothing to interfere, only the gentle breezes causing the wheat in the fields to sway in rhythmic unison against the backdrop of a blue sky. I would pray and then, since it was so quiet, listen for the Lord to respond. Actually, many times, He would speak to my heart first, initiating a conversation and waiting for my response to Him. I realized many years later that He understood my need for verbal communication, and this is how He reached me. After all, He made me a writer — communication is the lifeblood of writing. This is when my soul is most alive, with the interchange and interaction of words and meanings of words.

The Best Friend Ever

One day, while my heart was still walled in from all the pain and anger from my past, the Lord said something that began a meltdown in my heart. He said that He needed me and that I was unique and special to Him. He said that there was no one quite like me and that He was counting on me to be His friend. Well, I was floored! I searched the Scriptures to see what kind of God I was conversing with, to think that He wanted me to be His friend. I discovered that the Bible referred to very few people whom God actually called His friend. There was King David, and then in the New Testament, there were some of the disciples and other friends like Martha and Mary, but wow, wouldn't there have been crowds of people who would want to be God's friend? Not so. Over the course of the next few years, I came to realize that few people would seek out

God because they wouldn't think He would be interested in a friendship, that the personal cost was too high, and also because they are afraid of Him, like I used to be.

With this knowledge, the need for anger and self-centered pride melted away. In its place was a humbling and glad disposition. Also, I realized that there would be no more need for self-centered pride or to compete for the attention I thought I should have and deserved. I was important to Him, and I had a high calling to fulfill — befriend the King of Kings and Lord of Lords. What could top this? God was going to meet my needs for love and acceptance. He was raising up my level of importance; I didn't have to try on my own to prove how worthy or how good I was. But many years later, while I was in my late 20s, I had fallen prey to my sinful ways again and was struggling with anger and self-centered pride. This time, I would have a lot of house-cleaning to do.

In the next chapter, we are going to discuss how to clean up our act and what we need to do keep it clean, so that we can once again begin to enjoy our lives.

Chapter 3
A Clean House

We can't possibly enjoy freedom for very long if we continue to carry around baggage from a previous life that has enslaved us in some way. Even alcoholics must clean their cupboards and secret hiding places of any alcohol or bottles of liquor. While there are material things to dispose of, more often, it is our thoughts and behaviors that need cleaning up. It's interesting how you can think you have a clean enough house until someone comes over, only to discover that you really need to do a lot of cleaning up. Our lives work the same way. We think we are doing well until we are tested in an area that we come to realize is a weakness.

When I began attending the self-help group, I had no idea what my weaknesses were until I had to write them down. Notice I said "weaknesses," not "failures." These are areas where we could improve or get rid of altogether. For me, it was self-centered pride and also wanting to control things — my life, my environment, even the details surrounding my relationships. I discovered how common this is and that almost everybody struggles with the same thing. We want first place, and we want our lives to go in a certain way with nothing or no one to interfere. I had a lot of growing up to do, as well as giving up to do.

Coming Clean

In one of the steps in the program, we had to list all our hurts — everything we could think of for as far back as we could remember. Who hurt us, and what happened? But it didn't stop there. The real healing came when we had to write down our reaction to that hurt. Suddenly, my eyes were opened to the truth. I couldn't change what someone had done to hurt me, and I couldn't change what I had done in retaliation to them (even if it was revengeful thoughts). But it changed my attitude towards that person, and I realized that they are human, as I am, and they are weak, as I am, and that if I continue to hold a grudge against them, it is I who continues to suffer, and not them. The person being freed is me, not them. It is I who must forgive and then let it go. So I shared it all with a counselor, as suggested, then tore up the list and never thought about it ever again. I was truly free from all the hurts of my past. My heart and mind were uncluttered; my emotional and mental house was clean. It was like a rebirth. I could be and feel young again, light as a feather, happy as a bird let out of a cage.

A few years later, many things happened, and I struggled again with my emotions. This time it had to do with relationships, especially my relationship with God. For one thing, I was still single and really wanted to be married. I was in my early 30s, a time that is considered more difficult to find someone, and already surpassing a prime age as far as child-bearing goes. It was during these years that I struggled the most with my faith. Why wasn't God providing someone suitable? Unable to understand God's timetable, I often took matters into my own hands. This led to more trouble than I can mention, then soon I found myself back in a counselor's office, wondering why my life wasn't going the way I had planned or the way I would have liked it to go. This particular counselor uncovered a lot of baggage that went far back into my childhood. Unsettling things that had happened had affected how I viewed men. Hence, the need to control. The only person I trusted was myself. How can a relationship work unless you trust the other person?

Beware of Control

I'd like to talk about control. Control can lead to manipulation, and this can lead to witchcraft (see Galatians 5:19-26 for the works of the flesh). Witchcraft opens the door to satanic influence, which, once again, as mentioned in Chapter 1, puts us under bondage, and we will not be free. There are many ways a controlling spirit manifests. How do we know if we've crossed the line from wanting something or someone to be a certain way to actually being under the influence of a controlling spirit? Witchcraft is when a person manipulates another person to do what they want them to do. They may use guilt, threat, fear, obligation, or promise a reward (not a gift freely given). I am sure at one time or another we have all done this to try and get our own way. As children, we may have had a temper tantrum to get our own way. I know I did. It may or may not have worked. Some children are clever enough to use sympathy to try and get their own way. They appeal to a person's sense of pity.

In order for us to be free of trying to control others and of a controlling spirit, we must ensure we are under the divine authority of the Holy Spirit and that we have given Him full control of every area of our lives. I once had a platonic male friend that I depended on for spiritual fellowship. One day, he came over to my apartment and told me he felt that God didn't want him to be friends with me anymore. He believed that he had given me too much control over his life and that he had to break away so that he could find his own way without depending on me so much. I was shocked and very hurt, not realizing that he had felt this way. As far as I thought, he was a dear friend that I had enjoyed fellowship and friendship with. But he felt that he needed the time away so that he could develop a relationship with God that wasn't in any way influenced by me. So for about one year, he had nothing to do with me. Shortly after he told me, I handled it so badly that in my heart, out of anger and confusion, I rebelled against God. I wondered how God could take away a friend that I had shared so many of the same beliefs with, someone who challenged me in my faith and who I equally challenged. But I couldn't see into the future. God had a plan for my friend that would be far-reaching. He eventually went off to a Bible college and became a teacher there, reaching many young people and training them to go out into the world to share the Gospel and the Word that he so aptly taught.

In this case, I also had to let this friend and the friendship go, even though it was one of the most difficult things that had ever happened to me. I didn't understand why the complete separation, and so I reacted badly. But after I was able and willing to let my friend go, I was free to trust God to send along new friends that I could fellowship with. So, sometimes during this period of housecleaning, some relationships may end, and new ones begin.

Cleaning House

There is another way to clean house, other than getting rid of emotional baggage, and that is to literally examine our material things, the things that we own. Even in this area, the Lord also needs to have authority and be Lord of our material possessions. There are two things we need to consider. The first is that we literally go through our things and pray about what we need to throw away and get rid of completely. These things may be dragging us down spiritually and emotionally. They may have to do with cult icons, like certain records, books, pictures, and other paraphernalia. It may be letters from an old love, or it may be things from a past life that God has delivered us from, that may involve bad habits or things that aren't glorifying to God. Anything that leaves us with sadness, depression, or even a longing for former days gone by, probably needs to go. As difficult as this may be, it can be very freeing. Sometimes we hang onto things, thinking that they are good luck charms and will make our lives better. These things can become an idol, and our lives can't be blessed until we get rid of them.

When I was in my early 20s, a friend lovingly and insightfully pointed out to me that I was covetous. After the full realization hit me, I threw away most of the treasures of my past, including diaries, old tapes, a charm bracelet, clothes, books and things I could never get back again. It was very painful for me to do this, because these were all my childhood memories. Previous to this, whenever I did go back to my old diaries, there were some things and events that made me very sad, yet I still hung onto my past. But God assured me over and over again that He would restore the good memories, the ones I needed to remember when I would write my memoirs. And He has been faithful to do this for me. Throwing all these treasures away was very difficult, but it needed to be done so that I could move on in my life and look forward to making new memories.

I also had to throw away all my old rock-and-roll records and tapes from my teen years. I threw away all the posters, pictures, magazines, and so on that reminded me of a sinful past that I had once loved. God would have no competitors, even though these things were only material possessions. The point is, our possessions should never possess us. We must be willing to part with our things in order to truly be free from the power and hold they may have on us. While I don't believe in being superstitious, thinking there is a demon under every rock, I do believe that some things that are purchased carry with them a curse. Even the children of Israel were commanded to detest and destroy the idols of their enemies (see Deuteronomy 7:25-26, Exodus 23:24).

Covering with Prayer

Secondly, we need to pray over our dwelling places, workplaces, and even the ground we walk on or the highways we drive on. We need to pray over our homes, pray in each room for God to be there and sweep it clean of any unwelcome spirits that may oppress us unaware. When my husband and I stay in a hotel, we always pray over the room and the hotel that God be with us and sweep the room(s) clean of any unwelcome presence. When I was a student teacher in a large high school in the city, we did prayer walks around the school every night. I believe that this contributed to my success when I completed my two five-week teaching blocks. Where we live now, we go for prayer walks around our neighbourhood, both in the city and in the resort town where we own a house. In colder weather, we go for prayer drives and pray for people living in certain areas. This opens our eyes to many needs all around us, and it prepares the way for us and other faithful believers to minister to people later on in more tangible ways. An area must be cleaned up spiritually before God will work there. This is Scriptural as recorded in Exodus and Joshua. There are intercessory prayer groups all over the world praying for God's will to be done in strategic areas where Satan has had a long-time foothold, and where people are held captive by demonic influences.

So what happens when our spiritual and emotional house is clean? We then ask the Holy Spirit to dwell there and fill us with His Spirit, His righteousness and His thoughts. We give Him control over our hearts and lives, so that Satan cannot come back to influence us and oppress us. Many times, we will experience an immediate freedom from the oppression we have been under. When we clean our physical homes and get rid of unwanted stuff that is not glorifying to God and does us more harm than good, we also experience a freedom and a joy, because we are now unencumbered by things that have dragged us down. And when we pray over our homes, dwelling places, and our neighbourhood, etc., we start to see God work in miraculous ways, paving the way for future ministry, whereas before Satan had a foothold. An uncluttered life is a simple, joyful life. God honors our efforts to keep a clean house, making room for Him to dwell and to work.

In the next chapter, we're going to talk about three ways we communicate and explore the best way to communicate with others. We'll discover how to experience a new freedom in all of our relationships, rather than feel burdened, entrapped and/or weighed down by an unhealthy association with others. We'll even briefly discuss how to keep from becoming a burden to them.

Chapter 4
People Problems

Nowhere can we feel more enslaved than when it comes to our relationships with others. People problems or relationships affect us every day, whether we are single or married, with or without a family. Relationships especially affect us emotionally, since we are tied to people in one way or another and we are all interdependent on one another. We all know that many things can and do go wrong in relationships. Flare-ups and hurts are inevitable, although we'd all like to avoid them. We may wake up still angry at someone from the day before for something they said, did or didn't say or do. We may be fuming over an incident from an unfair boss or over-demanding parent, child, or spouse. We may be silently crying because a good friend or lover hurt us or rejected us. We may be so stressed out from the burdens others have placed on us that we feel we can't go on. Relationships both fulfil us and can drain us dry. We can't do without people in our lives, but sometimes we wish we could travel to an exotic desert island just to be alone for awhile. So how do we handle relationships without being enslaved by them?

Ways We Communicate

Many years ago, when I was still single and unemployed, I found out about a free community program that offered a job resume service, showed you how to find gainful employment, and also offered some psychology workshops.

One of the workshops was about communication and how to gain personal confidence, which would help you go forward from a depressing state of discouragement brought on by unemployment (and probably from job rejections) to a positive attitude where a company would be more likely to hire you. I was helped immeasurably by it. I learned, for instance, that we communicate in one of three ways — we are either being aggressive, passive, or assertive. Sometimes we are one or the other (aggressive or passive) depending on the situation, but a better way by far to communicate is by learning to be assertive.

We have all been aggressive, or have seen someone who is aggressive. That's when a person is angry, and you know about it right away. They tell you off without batting an eye, and then it's over and done with. Usually, we want to avoid someone like this, not wanting to be in their line of fire, always feeling attacked and tense, not knowing when they'll strike next. Then there's the passive person, opposite to the aggressive person, who, when upset with you, will give you the silent treatment rather than spew anger at you. They will likely keep everything inside, never letting you know how hurt, disappointed or upset they feel with you. If they feel really hurt, they may back off from you, and you won't hear from them for a long time, sometimes never. They may also use guilt and manipulation since they are afraid to confront you directly.

What is wrong with aggressive and passive behavior? Aggressive behavior is always destructive, leaving a path of broken hearts and injured people; passive behavior is equally destructive, resulting in withdrawal, sarcasm, bitterness, and even destructive gossip (rather than face the person who hurt them, they spread gossip about them to others). In addition, numerous health problems can arise from these two destructive ways of communicating (high blood pressure, stroke, arthritis, even cancer, and more). So by far, the best way to communicate is by being assertive.

The Right Way to Communicate

Assertiveness, I discovered, is learning to communicate in an open, honest, and direct way. It requires strength of character and wisdom, since rather than react instantly and negatively to someone else's unkind behavior towards you, you hold your emotions in check, sometimes wait, and first think about what your response will be. Unlike a passive response, you always respond, but carefully, openly, honestly, and directly.

What might this look like? An example is when a boss who owned a health food company I once worked for, openly ridiculed me and told me off for a mistake I made, and he did this in front of all the staff, who instantly sat up and took notice. I was mortified, stunned and embarrassed. Later, I gathered up my courage, went into his office, shut the door, and told him how I felt: that I realized I made the mistake, but telling me off in front of everyone made me feel embarrassed. He apologized and thanked me for sharing my true feelings. The secret to the success of my response is attributed to a technique that works almost every time, which has to do with the wording and the way in which it is said. Rather than starting the conversation with "you made me feel ...," which would have put him on the defensive, I started with, "I felt embarrassed." I could also say, "It made me feel embarrassed." I started with "I," not "you," and in doing this, I am only taking responsibility for my feelings, how what he said and did made me feel, not blaming him for making me feel embarrassed. There is a very big difference, although subtle.

Any conversation that starts with blaming the other person will end up in an argument, and nothing will be solved. Instead, we take ownership of our feelings and openly, honestly, and directly share how what they did or said made us feel. Nine times out of ten, people will respect us for handling things this way, and it will open up discussion in a non-threatening way. Often, it will mark the end of the disagreement or unpleasant situation, even though it may take some time. Being assertive requires thought and patience, but it always pays off if we will just take the time to control our emotions, calm down and wait until things settle. Most importantly, assertive behaviour is in agreement with Scripture:

> *A soft answer turneth away wrath: but grievous words stir up anger. Proverbs 15:1*

Learning Good Communication Skills

There is another positive spin-off from learning to communicate assertively — it instills self-confidence. You now become a person who can be trusted and respected as people come to realize you will not be emotionally swayed by disagreements or engage in mind games people sometimes play. For example, not too long after I took this course, my attitude changed, and I did find employment. Further, feeling encouraged and wanting to move forward with my life, I enrolled in a management program through continuing education at a local college. One of the courses

Chapter 4 - People Problems

intrigued me, and wanting to know even more about effectively communicating with people, I took a course called Assertiveness Training. The course was designed to give experience and knowledge in how to effectively communicate with people, especially co-workers and staff that you would one day be managing. I must have read about eight books on the subject, and I was so intrigued by what I learned that I felt that everyone should enroll in such a course. In many ways, it was life-changing because it changed the way I do things and think about things to this day. When someone offers you a better way to do something or think about something, you take it and make it your own. Soon, it becomes part of who you are and what you do.

There was a series of three books by the same author that I was particularly drawn to. A trained psychologist and public speaker, the author wrote a book about people and relationships, and how they can literally run your life and you may not even be aware of it. In fact, he devoted most of one of his books to discuss two things that will keep us from living a healthy and happy life — guilt and worry. While we struggle on our own with these two things (at least I did and still do at times), there are people in our lives who will especially use guilt to try to motivate us to do what they want at a great inconvenience and cost to us, which will make us feel like they are trying to control our lives. One of the most obvious instances is parents towards their children. Have you ever seen or known of a parent who keeps their grown children on a short leash? An elderly parent, may use guilt (even fear and threats) to keep a child running to and fro, back and forth to their aid even when they are able and capable of doing things for themselves. It is a control tactic that is completely self-centered on the part of the parent, especially if it keeps their children from living their own lives and caring for their own families. Children can be equally demanding on a parent, expecting to be taken care of when they could do much more for themselves.

The Enemy of Guilt

As if it isn't enough when people somehow make us feel guilty, we can also experience guilt of our own accord. But feeling guilty for our misdemeanors solves nothing. In fact guilt is not from God. God will convict us of our sin and misdemeanors and gently point out where we went astray; then when we repent of it, it's all over. God promises us He will not remember our sins any more (see Isaiah 43:25). But guilt without conviction and repentance on our part, amounts to a waste of time and energy. The quickest way to be rid of guilt is to do good and not dwell on our faults and failures. If we feel guilty for something and we can fix it, we need to do everything possible to make it right. This is especially true if we know we have hurt someone in some way. We need to make things right with that person and try and restore the relationship. If we are not doing something we know we should do, we need to start doing it. It might even be as simple as completing a project we started and didn't finish that someone is waiting for. It may be not returning important calls, or calling friends in need when we know we should even though we're busy. We may need to do many things, but we need to start somewhere. Even just beginning to do one pressing thing will re-activate us and put us on the right path and on the way to restored sanity and fruitfulness once again.

When Worry Assails Us

Worry is another peace stealer. If we aren't feeling bad or guilty about something, we may be worrying about something. These are two pesky negative things that can and will fill our minds if we let them. We may be worried about finances, our health, upcoming doctors' appointments, relationships, our spouses, parents or kids. We may worry about our future, whether we will be or remain gainfully employed, whether our health holds up, the weather and how it affects our lifestyles, or any number of events, like flying or taking a trip to a faraway destination. Maybe we are worrying because we have overextended ourselves and we're already stressed out. We don't have the strength to fight our fears as we usually do.

The author of the three books I read suggested that worry and guilt are really a clever way for us to avoid the present. Guilt keeps us in the past, and worry keeps us in the future; therefore, we can escape the many cares of the day that require our attention. I had never seen things this way before. In order to live in the present, I must rid myself of guilt and worry. If I attend to the things of today only, I will have no room for guilt and worry. Better yet, if I accept God's forgiveness (and others and myself), and thank Him for His quick willingness to continue loving me unhindered, my attitude will change, and I will see myself as He sees me, free and forgiven. And if I prayerfully plan for a bright and cheery future and believe God for it, my present day will be that much more enjoyable. Guilt and worry will have no place in my life, since I will take on more practical ways to deal with these negative emotions, namely by taking some kind of positive action. Most of all, God has provided a way for us to live carefree no matter what happens, and that is to live by faith in Him and in His many promises. We have a much bigger God, bigger than all of our problems combined. He is there for us and will see us through any and every situation. When we trust in Him, He promises us peace that only He can give (see John 14:27).

Healthy Relationships

Having said all this, what makes a healthy relationship, and how can we best be a friend to others without becoming a bothersome burden to them and also enslaving them? I believe it all has to do with our level of dependency on others. Do we lean too much on others rather than take our burdens to the Lord? Are we independent, helpful, cheerful and willing to bend our self-made rules a little? Do we listen more than talk? Are we open to change, or in some cases, drop our rigid schedule enough to let people in even when they show up at our door unannounced?

Our life in the small resort town we live in is like that. There is an easy, relaxed atmosphere, and people aren't at all stressed out like they are in the city. We often drop by to see a friend or a neighbour, especially in the summer months when people are outside in their yards or enjoying a campfire on a cool spring or summer night. There is no such thing as "party crashing." The more people show up, the better. There is a friendly camaraderie, where we are all enjoying the relaxed life at the beach. When people are relaxed, they are happier, and fewer arguments unfold. We see this especially true in marriages. That's why a weekend away to a nice hotel or resort on a regular basis

Chapter 4 - People Problems

could possibly save many marriages from disaster if couples would just take the time for each other.

In the next chapter, we're going to discuss how to handle our sometimes greatest enemy to freedom and fulfillment in life, and that is ourselves.

Footpath to Freedom

Chapter 5
The Problem With Self

With all the talk about self-love and self-esteem, is it any wonder we are narcissistic and overly concerned about ourselves? We live in a humanistic society obsessed with the worship of self. Yet, humanists, who extol the lordship of "self," have done us no favors; but rather, their line of thinking has turned us away from the only answer to our freedom. Eve, unwittingly, was the first humanist, wanting a knowledge that was outside of God's plan for us. This act puts self on the throne of our lives, rather than God. This disobedient act was pride rising up in all its ugly, self-glory. But God condemned such an act and cursed the ground Adam walked on, and caused a separation from God that only sacrifice by death and atonement could repair. Jesus Christ was sent to restore us back to God when He died on the cross to forgive us of our sins.

Ever since the first sin in the Garden of Eden, we have struggled with self and sinful pride. Rather than live by faith and divine understanding, we now struggle with fear, doubt and misunderstanding. You see it in every relationship. You may feel it in waking up every morning, encumbered by the many cares of each day. Knowledge without God is a terrible burden, and so is sinful flesh if we allow it to rule our thoughts and actions. Self can be our number one enemy, keeping us from enjoying life, relationships, and the freedom God provides for us only through His Son, Jesus Christ.

Discerning Who We Are

Also, we may spend our lives confused about who we are. We may think that we know ourselves, but then we discover things that we didn't know at all. Not only has sin blinded us, but I believe God created us in such a way that we never really completely know ourselves. We may know what we like and dislike, but this isn't enough information to live a fruitful, happy and contented life. We will stumble time and again on this frail path of self-knowledge that is so limited and may change day by day. Again, our sinful nature stands in the way of true enlightenment, because we really can't see our true selves without divine revelation. We keep trying to live a spiritual life, something we all strive for, which has nothing to do with religion, by using the means of the flesh.

Clearly, flesh and spirit are two completely different things. We can only know spiritual things (like who we really are) with spiritual means. I believe this is God's way of turning our attention towards Him because He knows we need Him to reveal our true selves and show us the path we must take throughout our lives. Of course, many people choose to turn away from God, and so stumble through life, then discover after life that they've made a grave mistake and are now forever separated from God. The Apostle Paul said that we (this means believers in Christ) will only truly know who we are in the future, when we meet the Lord face to face:

> *For now we see through a glass, darkly; but then face to face: now I know in part; but then shall I know even as also I am known.*
> *1 Corinthians 13:12*

Prideful Self

One of the stumbling blocks that keeps us from seeing our true selves, as mentioned earlier, is pride, which, in its unhealthy state, causes us to have an over-inflated view of ourselves. How does pride manifest itself? It's when we are overly sensitive and feel injured easily. It's when we are overbearing and always right, making others feel crushed. It is when we have given too much thought to ourselves and not enough thought to others. We can go through life feeling persecuted and rejected, and other people may not even be aware. This is self, working overtime to get attention, and puts an unfair demand on others to bend to our emotional swings. Self is deceived by sin and can never provide an accurate picture of what is really going on inside.

While a student in Bible school, the picture of my true self was revealed to me. I had rebelled against God and had a good idea why, but God went beyond this surface understanding and showed me things I never would have known. At the heart of my rebellion was the feeling that I wasn't as good as others and that there was no use for me. Feeling rejected and worthless, I acted out what I believed about myself. If I am worthless, then what does it matter what I do? No one will notice or care anyway. Can you see the self-pity in this? This is really the flip side of the same coin called pride. We are either over-inflated or under-inflated. It is all about self-centered pride. Was I thinking beyond my own hurts, of how I might be a blessing to others and forget about myself and my own personal woes? Was I thankful for all my blessings that God had provided? No. I was too blinded by self to see any good, and so I had an inaccurate picture of what was really going on. Only Jesus can set us free from the prison of self, and the misunderstanding it creates to imprison us.

Judging & Being Judged

Another thing a prideful spirit does is to be overly concerned about what is fair and what is unfair. It rises up, and judges others without knowing the whole story. Have you ever been unfairly judged? I'm sure we all have. It's like someone sneaking up behind you and hitting you over the head. You didn't see it coming, and you're shocked by the impact of it. I've had people judge me for things I didn't even know I had done. Sometimes when people are angry about something, they take it out on you since you're the closest target. They aren't really angry at you, but rather than deal with the real issue that troubles them, they camouflage it and attack you instead. We see this every day in traffic. With so much road rage, people honk their horns because someone has cut them off and even drive dangerously because they're emotionally out of control. We see it in a marriage, where couples are tired and overstressed, then attack each other for little apparent reason. Sometimes a boss will explode for no apparent reason, like what happened to me at the health food company. Without knowledge, the Bible says, we are fools (see Proverbs 12:23, 13:16).

In my case, I rebelled, partly because I was comparing myself to others. This led me down a hopeless path of never being good enough, so why try in the first place? Also, as long as I wasn't good enough, I could gracefully bow out of taking responsibility for many things in life. I could always leave it up to someone else who could do a better job than me. But there is no fulfillment in this line of thinking, and no adventure in learning or trying new things. One day, I read the following verse, and this began a big change in my life:

> *But let every man prove his own work, and then shall he have rejoicing in himself alone, and not in another. Galatians 6:4*

If I put everything into what God has given me, I will be satisfied with my own work and not be envious or compare myself with others. This has been proven many times over. When I write a book, I pray about it, and then write it to the best of my own ability. When I do a painting, I do it with an abandon, pushing aside convention and painting it to my own liking. If I like or love my work, I know others will too. It takes courage to live up to your own convictions. Also, I have since learned that God created us all unique. We are not to copy-cat anyone, but remain true to who God made us.

The Problem with Self-Esteem

What we truly believe about ourselves will either make us or break us. We need to have a healthy, realistic view of who we are. We can be persuaded by low self-esteem, but on the other hand, we can have too much self-esteem. Society has put so much emphasis on self-esteem and self-love that it has done more harm than good, especially when it comes to how we raise and teach our children. And in the past few years, it has increasingly gotten worse. Without a healthy balance and knowledge of our own inherent sinful nature and the destruction it brings, children have no guidelines for what is right and wrong. They think they can get away with anything. You have only to read the headlines in the newspaper to see that they are even getting away with murder. Without discipline for the wrong they are doing, they have no boundaries, and are out of control to the detriment of everyone else. Society must now pay for its too liberal and ill-conceived views on how or even *if* we discipline our children.

How Self Traps Us

Many years ago, when I started researching the topic of backsliding, I found a verse in the Bible that really explained to me how self can trap us and enslave us:

> ***The backslider in heart shall be filled with his own ways: and a good man shall be satisfied from himself. Proverbs 14:14***

I thought back to the many years I had lived for myself, giving little thought to others and how I might be hurting them. I was selfish and thought mostly of myself. I know that my parents worried about me, not knowing where I was many times. When we are backslidden, we don't realize how we affect the people around us. Alcoholics, for example, destroy themselves and everyone around them. They can have despicable behavior that embarrasses a spouse and children, inflicts untold emotional and physical pain, and will even cost them a marriage, their job, their health, and so on. What we do does matter, and it directly affects others either positively or negatively. While backslidden, I thought I was free and living an exciting life, trying daring things and testing fate. But anything driven by sin is a trap that enslaves us and eventually leads to death. This is written in the Bible:

> *Enter ye in at the strait gate: for wide is the gate, and broad is the way, that leadeth to destruction, and many there be which go in thereat:*
> *Matthew 7:13*

Taking on Others' Problems

In the self-help group I attended, it was suggested many times to stop taking on the responsibility of other's sins, and especially trying to change them. This helped me immeasurably, because I had just come out of a bad relationship with someone who could have destroyed my life. I found out too late that he was involved in drugs and was also an alcoholic. I thought I could change him, so I tried everything in my power to keep him from these things. I nearly had a nervous breakdown in the process. I stopped eating, and I was so exhausted that I could barely make it to work every day. I was trying to perform a balancing act — believing he was the right one, I thought if I could just keep him on the straight and narrow, then everything would magically fit into place. So I would have one victory, only to discover he would quickly fail me in another. Even if he changed to suit me, how would I know his change would be permanent?

Alcoholics tend to be up and down — on and off the wagon intermittently their whole lives. Something might set him off to go back to drinking. I would never have the peace and assurance that he was completely cured. Drugs gave him a split personality, as well. When he was free from the drugs and alcohol, he was peaceful, happy and a joy to be with. But when he went back on them, he was agitated, ornery and short-tempered. What kind of a life was I getting myself into? Thankfully, a very wise counselor told me straight where the relationship was heading, and I decided to break it off with him. I'm so thankful every day since that I did so.

How to Be Free

The way to freedom is to deal with self, not to try to change everyone and everything else around us. This is tremendously freeing. This doesn't mean we stop caring about others; it means that once we deal with our own issues, we have more grace and more room in our lives to give more of ourselves to others in need. Our joy from the freedom we experience will become infectious, and others will be drawn to us, rather than feel uncomfortable by our many demands that they change for our sake. Ultimately, to continue a free lifestyle, we need to commit everything to the Lord Jesus Christ and make Him Lord of our lives. Earlier, I said that we don't really know ourselves, much less know anyone else. But Jesus created us, and He knows us intimately. He even knows the number of hairs on our head (see Matthew 10:30). He alone offers freedom from self, for He nailed our sinful nature to the cross when He died for our sins:

> *Knowing this, that our old man is crucified with him, that the body of sin might be destroyed, that henceforth we should not serve sin. Romans 6:6*
>
> *I am crucified with Christ: nevertheless I live; yet not I, but Christ liveth in me: and the life which I now live in the flesh I live by the faith of the Son of God, who loved me, and gave himself for me. Galatians 2:20*

Think of it—the very things of the flesh we struggle with every day have no power over us once we refuse to give in to them. Read the above verses over again. Read them every day and every time you have a thought or struggle that seems insurmountable. We are indeed free from self and the demands of our own sinful nature. Knowing this is enough to keep us humble and dependent on the Lord to continue to lead us out of our entrapments into the freedom and joy He offers us. For even though He has set us free, our sinful nature will still try to control us. This is where faith and taking a determined stand against it will keep us walking in that freedom.

In the next chapter, we'll look at ways to view hardships as stepping stones to much greater things.

Footpath to Freedom

Chapter 6
From Hardships to Plenty

Have you ever had so many bad things happen to you that you believed you were a target of the cosmos, destined for disaster no matter what you did? We have all had days, weeks, and seasons when we feel that nothing is going right and possibly never will. Some people believe this is the luck of the draw or fate playing sadistic games with us. We may stop believing in anything good and get so down we can hardly pull up our bootstraps. I can tell you that if anyone would have had the right to feel discouraged, it was Job in the Bible. When things are piling up on you, you should read through Job. It's extremely enlightening. Even though Satan had God's permission to tempt and try Job, Job never lost his confidence in the goodness of God. That's pretty impressive and also provides us with answers.

Did you know that God loves to take impossible things and work them out so magnificently and so elaborately that we could never even begin to imagine how He does it? His excellent ways are past finding out, as the following indicates:

> *For my thoughts are not your thoughts, neither are your ways my ways, saith the LORD. For as the heavens are higher than the earth, so are my ways higher than your ways, and my thoughts than your thoughts. Isaiah 55:8-9*

This truth came to me, but at a great cost, since it was going to take quite a few years to see God's hand at work in some major areas of my life. Many years ago, when I was still a teenager on the brink of turning 20, I couldn't seem to find direction for my life, and I often felt confused about which way to go. I was living at home and working part-time as a waitress in a busy downtown restaurant. I could barely pay for the gas in my car, let alone make monthly payments on it. My parents kindly offered free room and board, and this greatly helped, but spending money was scarce, and I couldn't very well plan for a future without a decent job. I was tithing at the time and believed that God would provide through my faithfulness in giving to His work. One time, I gave a whole hard-earned paycheck from my waitressing job to a ministry that had greatly helped me. I thought that God would immediately provide me with a better job and He'd shower me with financial blessings, but that never happened. Instead, I was to struggle through hardships for another two years or so before I saw the hand of God at work.

An Open Door

Through a series of events, I got laid off from my waitressing job and, after much prayer and seeking God, felt that He was directing me to move to Winnipeg and live with my sister, who needed me at the time. I got a job in an office almost immediately and moved in with my sister. But this job proved to be too much for me, so I quit on the spot. It was summer, and my parents, my sister, and her small boy (a toddler) were taking the train to Vancouver Island to visit my relatives. I wanted to go, so I started selling cosmetics and cleaning products door-to-door to make enough money to at least pay my train fare there and

Chapter 6 - From Hardships to Plenty

back. But the trip didn't solve a thing. I worried every minute about finding another job when I returned to Winnipeg. Once I returned to Winnipeg, I was given a lead to a job opening in a large department store nearby the apartment where we lived. Then, a couple of months later, another job opportunity arose. I was called in for an interview to work for a newspaper as **the** editor of a new publication they were launching. It was my dream job, and I was so thrilled, because writing was my career and my love. I had been trained for this kind of work. So I got hired and quit the department store job. For four months, I enjoyed the autonomy and great interest of being out interviewing people, writing stories and hiring other writers to fill the pages. The first issue came out, and then my boss came in to my office to inform me that the second issue would not be coming out because they didn't have enough advertising to pay for the paper (which was offered free to readers). He offered no other job opening. I was devastated. Now what would I do? Go back to the department store or waitressing? I had already tasted the joy and excitement of writing, of getting my work published, and getting paid for it. What could top this?

Closed Doors

It took awhile, but I was to learn that God does not deal in the carnal or the natural. He is not persuaded or moved by the demands and desires of the flesh. God's ways are always spiritual first, and He uses the things of the world to bring glory to Himself and to fulfil His plans for our lives. For some reason, the unemployment insurance cheques I was to receive were not forthcoming, and neither was a job. For six long and trying months, I was unemployed with no hope of receiving any money, other than what I borrowed from my parents and my kind sister, who had a heart of gold and never let me go without a meal. During this time, I kept applying for paying writing jobs, but nothing came up. With time to spare, I continued my personal writing, in hopes that perhaps I could write short stories or even novels that would sell, and I could make a living at it. But I kept coming back to the Bible, and I used it as a means to find answers to the many hardships I was facing. In fact, I had learned how to study it and was writing what I was learning as I read. This began a lifetime of searching the Scriptures for answers to life's problems, which would later become the source of some of the material I'd share in my books; yet, still, I was young, impressionable, and had much to learn.

One day, my sister, seeing my despair, depression and despondency from so many months of unemployment, gave me God-inspired advice. She knew that I wanted to write, and yet nothing was opening up for me in that area, so she said that she believed that if I would humble myself and take any job I could find, God would honor me with the time to write to my heart's content. I knew she was right and that it was the right thing to do. So I started applying everywhere, even at gas stations to pump gas. Through my course of travels, one day I went into a large department store and started talking to the lady behind the jewelry counter. I told her my predicament and that I had always wanted to work for the railway (as well as writing, I loved traveling). She said that her husband and her son work for Via Rail, a passenger train company subsidized by the government. She said she might be able to pass my name along when they were hiring again. I knew how hard it was to get a job working for the railway unless you had strong connections, but I gave her my name and number anyway, not thinking for a moment that anything more would come of it.

A Turn-Around

One day, the phone rang. It was the gas station asking me to come in for an interview. They had an opening. I could work evenings behind the window and just collect money from people since it was a self-serve gas bar. I could bring along a book to read and even get in some writing when it was slow. But at the back of my mind was a growing fear — I would be working at night, alone, in a gas bar in an almost obscure area of the city. But God had opened this door, and I must trust Him to protect me, so I agreed to come in for the interview. The pay wasn't bad either — more than minimum wage to start. An hour or so after I agreed to come in for the interview, I got another phone call. It was personnel from Via Rail asking me to come in for a typing test. They had an opening in their reservations department. I was stunned and thrilled and couldn't wait to tell my sister! If I could pass the typing test, I would have a good-paying government job even though they said it was only for the summer. I can't remember if I passed the typing test or not, but the man who hired me was the husband of the lady I had met at the jewelry counter in the large department store months earlier. She had remembered me! Isn't God good?

When I got my first paycheque, I had never seen so much money at one time. Soon, I was able to pay off my debts to my sister, parents and others who had been lending me money. I obtained credit immediately based on my hourly wage and was able to purchase things I needed, like clothing and food. I could get my car insured and afford to put gas in without penny-pinching and having to take the bus or walk. I remembered back to the time when I had sent in my whole paycheck for God's work. God never forgot about me. He was showing me how miraculously He works. This job provided the impetus that would one day open up the writing career my heart longed for. But it would also be a long way off.

I learned from this experience that God has a perfect timing for everything significant that happens in our lives. I was impatient, wanting everything to happen right away, in **my** time. But God wanted me to learn to trust in Him and show me how all these seemingly negative events are all leading to a far-reaching miracle that God has been orchestrating all along.

God at Work

There were two significant life-changing events that happened. I made a friend who was struggling with his sexuality and also had a drug problem, both of which resulted in nervous problems. After many months of witnessing to him about God's love and power to change us, he gave his life to Christ, and God made all things new for him. He was the kind of charismatic personality that touches people's lives and, infectiously, draws people to Christ with his enthusiasm. He ended up in Bible School, married and has two children. His ministry affected thousands of students through the years. God works in ways that give Him the most glory, only I never could have dreamed He would use me to help this young friend I met while working for the railway.

Chapter 6 - From Hardships to Plenty

A Miracle Unfolds

    Another big, exciting, life-changing event was meeting the man I would one day marry. Craig worked in the stores and also as a red-cap. I worked in the ticket office, having switched from the reservations department, where you don't actually meet your public face-to-face. Now I was meeting all kinds of people, and I just loved this job, selling tickets, giving directions, announcing train arrivals and departures, taking in money from on-board services, meeting the conductors, engineers and various train staff. I also had a free pass and made several trips all over Canada using my pass.

    Craig used to come up to the ticket counter and chat whenever the trains were late, and there was nothing else to do. One evening, Craig offered to give me a ride home since he lived close by with his parents in the south end of the city. I would have had to take a bus or walk a ways to the nightclub where my sister was working, wait for her to get off work, and get a ride home with her. My car must have been in the repair shop at the time. I really appreciated the ride home.

    After a few years, I knew I wanted to move on and work in sales so I could be out of the office more, so I quit the railway job and got hired to sell newspaper advertising. But still, writing was the calling and career I was aiming for. Eventually, I ended up working for the government full-time, which gave me the stability of a 9- to-5 schedule, evenings and weekends free, and also paid for my way through university. After six long years of night school and summer school, I completed 15 courses and earned my Bachelor of Arts degree, majoring in English.

God Fulfills My Dreams

Several years passed, and my dream of writing still seemed so far away. Then one day, I saw Craig at a local grocery store we both shopped in. He was still single and said he was going to university, taking computer science. I needed a computer, so he offered to help me pick one out. For five years (now a total of 15 years since we first met at the railway), we were friends, phoning each other and going out for meals and movies. Nothing more than a platonic friendship had developed until the fifth year of our friendship. God was working on me, preparing me for a huge step, and working on Craig to join me in taking that step. Craig started attending the same church as me and quietly inquired about my faith. By the fall of that 15th year, we fell in love with each other, knew God had brought us together, and were married within four weeks of dating. A few months later, I quit my job and began the writing career my sister had said God would open up to me all those years before.

Many times when we are assailed with bad things, God is always working things out behind the scenes, intricately working out all the details of our complicated (to us) prayer requests and according to His plan for our lives. The things we have no control over, we have to trust God for. **The bad things in our lives sometimes must happen in order for us to bear fruit that is eternal and everlastingly rewarding.** We may not like crossing bridges, but in order to get over to the other side where the fulfilment of our dreams await, we must step forward, not look down, and also face the many fears we may encounter along the way. The many rich blessings of the Lord will be our reality, no matter what happens along the way, because we trust wholeheartedly in

God. Once we pass the many tests that seem to impede our progress, God opens doors, and we are free to pursue and enjoy our deepest heart's desires.

In the next chapter, we'll discover how to strategically direct our thoughts to deliberately find success in reaching our goals and experience positive outcomes for our lives.

Footpath to Freedom

Chapter 7
Strategic Thinking

Everything we do and almost everything that happens to us are direct results of how we think. We can be negative and not even realize it, and then negative things happen to us as a result. I'd like to share a situation that happened to my husband and me regarding this. One Friday evening in the early fall, my husband and I had come through a very hectic week in the city, and we were driving out to our house at the lake as we did every Friday. We hadn't taken a holiday for two years, were feeling overtired, and it felt like we were doing the same thing over and over again, and not really accomplishing very much. I had been writing one book after another with little break in between, and then publishing them myself at home. My husband was mentioning that he hadn't had time to work on a project on the computer for over a year since the time he was first inspired by the idea, and we were both excited about it.

We both felt very strongly that the completion of my books and his project would lead us into ministry, where we could travel and spread the Gospel of the good news, without him having to worry about quitting his job and then raising our own funds to do so. But here we were, months later, and except for the completion of some of my books, no further ahead. Feeling discouraged, we felt that maybe my husband should just forego the idea of writing his computer project, since he could never seem to find the time to do it, and I would just continue writing the books until the Lord directed me to do otherwise. So we left it at that, not happy with the decision, but not knowing what else to do.

Words of Encouragement

Later that night, the phone rang. It was my dear uncle from the West Coast. He asked how we were doing, and we told him things were okay. Then he started ministering to us and did so for a full hour. It wasn't until later that I told him how discouraged we had been feeling about my husband's project and that we felt he should put it aside. Also, I told him that even though I was writing the books, I had no financial means to publish them properly, but I would continue to write them until the Lord led me to do otherwise. Everything he had said to us, even before he knew how we were feeling, we knew, was directly given to him from the Lord Jesus to encourage us not to give up what we were doing and wanted to do. He quoted many Scriptures and told us to read Deuteronomy 28. **So later we read those verses and discovered the secret to every success in life—we must first obey God, and then His promises will begin to unfold.** To quit a good work for the kingdom of God would be to disobey what He had given us to do. He also gave us a verse to use when discouragement or anything contrary to God's Word assails us:

> *Submit yourselves therefore to God. Resist the devil, and he will flee from you. James 4:7*

I realized that all that week before, I had not slept a single night. Either I was having bad dreams, or I was so stressed and worried about things, I couldn't get to sleep. Fatigue opens the door for Satan to come and whisper his poisonous, untrue lies in our ears. I had allowed him to do so by not taking my cares to the Lord. Strategic thinking must be Bible-based and God-based. We must take a deliberate stand against every lie of Satan, and instead fill our minds with the true Word of God. God's Word is very powerful and will defeat every foe.

Beware of the Source

We may think that troublesome thoughts are a result of our own fatigue, which sometimes they are, but often this is not the case at all. A friend once shared with me that she was asked to sing in a church as a guest. Although she has sung many times before in front of an audience, this particular time she was feeling very nervous about it. I felt I should pray for her and remind her that fear is not of God, and those thoughts were popped in from Satan to torment her. She took it to heart and later shared with me that she did pray strategically, and the fear and nervousness she felt earlier were completely gone. She was set free and able to sing joyfully and in praise to God. The following verses attest that our thought life can be a battleground, and we need to be vigilant to fight against these unwelcome attacks:

> *(For the weapons of our warfare are not carnal, but mighty through God to the pulling down of strong holds;) Casting down imaginations, and every high thing that exalteth itself against the knowledge of God, and bringing into captivity every thought to the obedience of Christ; 2 Corinthians 10:4-5*

How do we know when our thinking is right? After my uncle called and gave us so many wonderful Scriptures filled with the promises of our loving God, I realized that our thinking is right when it is filled with faith in God. When I am thinking positive, I am believing in God and in His many promises. When I am filled with joy, excitement and happy anticipation, I am filled with faith in God. When I am negative, depressed and unhappy, I have been listening to the lies of Satan. Clearly, fear is not of God, but God is a God of love:

> *For God hath not given us the spirit of fear; but of power, and of love, and of a sound mind.*
> *2 Timothy 1:7*
>
> *There is no fear in love; but perfect love casteth out fear: because fear hath torment. He that feareth is not made perfect in love. 1 John 4:18*
>
> *Let your conversation be without covetousness; and be content with such things as ye have: for he hath said, I will never leave thee, nor forsake thee. So that we may boldly say, The Lord is my helper, and I will not fear what man shall do unto me.*
> *Hebrews 13:5-6*

Fear vs. Faith Thoughts

Fearful thoughts paralyze us. Faith-filled thoughts propel us forward with great joy and determination. Fear is when we are unsure of something and are perplexed about what to do. Faith is when we are sure of something (according to Hebrews 11:1) and move forward boldly. In the above verse, we have a powerful promise of God — He has promised never to leave us or forsake us. The night that my uncle called us, it was as if the Lord had heard every word and had felt every sorrow we had felt, and prompted my uncle to call and minister to us. One of the things my uncle assured us is that the Lord is never far away. He hears our hearts' cries and understands our deepest needs. He will never forsake us, and will open every door and answer every prayer, even if we only ask once. He shared with us that, like a parent who hears the request of their child the first time and then plans to fulfil that desire, so does God hear us the first time and then make plans to fulfil our request (see Matthew 7:9-11).

We cannot move forward in our lives and fulfil our tasks and dreams that God has placed in our hearts, unless we really believe God will work things out to enable them to happen. Why is it good to have goals and dreams? It establishes our thoughts and gives us a direction to move towards. We have peace of mind because we stop wondering what to do and where to go. When I take a trip, I first plan for it. I look up the best places to go, where to stay, look up interesting things to see and do, and, finally, look at maps to learn the best routes if we are driving there. I have tremendous peace of mind when I know where I am going and that when I get there, I'll have a nice place to stay. Yet many times, dreams and goals don't always work out so smoothly. They have not always happened when I wanted them to, nor were they handed to me on a silver platter. Mostly, I had to wait, sometimes many years, before I saw my dreams fulfilled, especially the desire to get married, as I shared in the previous chapter.

Submitting to God

Further, it always seems that in my case, I've had to give over my dreams, my heart, and every thought of my plans to the Lord before He can unlock the doors and make things happen. I know He has asked me to do this on several occasions because I had become both obsessive and possessive of my dreams, insisting that seeing my dreams fulfilled was the only way I would be fulfilled. But He has had to challenge me to give them over to Him and instead, promise to love Him and serve Him no matter what, even if my dreams are never fulfilled the way and when I want them to be. Many years ago, when I was thinking I would like to get married, the Lord gave me a verse that has stayed with me:

> **Delight thyself also in the LORD; and he shall give thee the desires of thine heart. Psalm 37:4**

This is a completely different turn in thinking. When I am thankful for what I have already, God gives me peace and contentment, and I'm not driven away from Him by focusing on the desires of my heart. When I praise Him, I am acknowledging how good He is to me and how excellent His ways are. I am submitting my carnal thinking and sinful flesh to the waste-basket of thinking, and I am tuning in to the greatest Mind possible, the mind of Christ. What a tremendous privilege to know the Lord and be in His presence through prayer and worship, and have access to all the wisdom that He freely gives to His beloved children who ask.

The Right Focus

When I first started studying the Bible in my teen years, I was always drawn to Romans 8. It is one of my favorite, most well-loved chapters in the whole Bible. I didn't really understand it all, but the following verses really intrigued me, and I've thought about them many times since:

> *For to be carnally minded is death; but to be spiritually minded is life and peace. Because the carnal mind is enmity against God: for it is not subject to the law of God, neither indeed can be. So then they that are in the flesh cannot please God.* **Romans 8:6-8**

What exactly is a carnal mind? I believe it means that it's when we are focused on the flesh and the appetites of our body. When we focus on the flesh and our old nature, we are concerned about something that is already dead or can bring no life. To be spiritually minded is to enjoy a peace that can only be known by the spiritual part of us. But in order for this to work, we have to be indwelt by the Holy Spirit, who alone gives life and peace. What should be the basis of our thoughts? Anything that is in agreement with Scripture should be our focus. Scripture brings us life and will give us peace and contentment. The only way to align our thoughts with Scripture is by reading the Bible and prayerfully asking God to reveal His thoughts to us. A mind without the knowledge or direction of God is a reprobate mind, opposed to the very nature of God Himself. This is the "enmity" the above verses refer to.

A Clear Focus

In my early 20s, my oldest sister used to send me greeting cards to encourage me. I knew she cared about me and was praying for me. She was and is a constant support to me, a source of encouragement, and I appreciate her so much. She had two favorite verses that she always quoted when she'd send me a beautiful card with a note inside:

> **Trust in the LORD with all thine heart; and lean not unto thine own understanding. In all thy ways acknowledge him, and he shall direct thy paths.**
> **Proverbs 3:5-6**

During those earlier years when I was just starting out on my own, I struggled a lot with making decisions. Where should I go and what should I do? By the time I was 24, many of my friends were getting married, and I felt like I was left in the dust with no marriage partners in sight. I really wanted to write for a living, but jobs were hard to come by. So I applied for clerical and or sales jobs, both jobs I could do well. But since I wasn't really fulfilled in my jobs, I suffered with a lot of unhappiness, and wondered why God was not answering my prayers. At such times, I would be reminded of the above two verses and would apply them as best as I could. I'd re-focus my thoughts and try not to think so much about how unhappy I was feeling or how I could escape the mundane life I felt I was leading. But when I prayed, that's when I noticed the big difference. God used these times to teach me many things about myself and the path He was leading me on.

They were very specific lessons about money, relationships, emotions, and even my dreams. Thinking back now, those were leisurely times, and God expanded my outlook and my thinking. One by one, He would open a window and reveal something more. Day by day He would provide for my needs. Times spent with Him were my best times, and contentment and hope would fill my heart. If He had provided what I wanted most — a companion and a writing career, I never would have known Him as I do now, and I never would have known contentment and peace as I do now.

Thoughts & Obedience

One day, when I was reading the Bible, the Lord directed me to another wonderful verse about our thinking:

> **Commit thy works unto the LORD, and thy thoughts shall be established. Proverbs 16:3**

This was a profound revelation, and one that I had to let deeply sink in. For one thing, I had to ask myself, **Was I praying about my day and the many things I had on my list to do? Was I doing my own thing or was I truly listening for the instruction of the Lord?** If I was burned out and doing too much, was I really doing what the Lord had asked me to do? I wouldn't know this unless I had prayed and asked God for some direct answers. So I had to learn to get into my prayer closet, be quiet, and listen for the Lord. It takes humility to be quiet, not say anything, and then wait. It takes discipline to make an effort to pray about things. This is when we need to be very demanding of our flesh and put it in its rightful place (see I Corinthians 9:27). This is when we no longer submit to the demands of our flesh, but take control of it and do what God's spirit within us wills. And we need to do this every day, perhaps many times a day.

The thoughts from the Lord are clear and easy to understand. They are not mixed with any untruths or doubts (see James 3:17). The more we read His Word, the more transformed our thoughts will be, as it says in Romans 12:2:

> *And be not conformed to this world: but be ye transformed by the renewing of your mind, that ye may prove what is that good, and acceptable, and perfect, will of God.*

May we strive for this mind, and keep our thoughts strategic and focused, not falling into the traps of the enemy.

In the next chapter, we will look further at exploring new thought patterns and look at creative ways to think outside the box.

Chapter 8
Exploring New Territory

There are three ways we are going to look at to begin a new life of freedom, especially in our thinking, and each one provides an open door for us to begin exploring new territory. They are:

1. Rid our minds of fear
2. Become proactive in arming ourselves with faith
3. Deliberately explore new thoughts and ideas

1. Rid Our Minds of Fear

In the last chapter, we briefly talked about fear. Now we'll elaborate on it. We can live in fear, and it can determine all of our thoughts and our actions, or more likely, inaction, in the way we approach life and new situations. Fear is behind most of our anxieties. In fact, fear is the father of anxiety. Fear comes camouflaged in many subtle ways, ways we sometimes cannot detect until we are at our wits' end and someone or God must intervene on our behalf. You could almost say we are possessed by fear because it keeps us from living a life of freedom that God wants us to live.

Maybe some people don't realize this, but when Jesus died on the cross, He not only took our sins, sicknesses, sorrows and all the effects that sin produces, but He also took all our fears upon Himself. The Bible says that fear torments us, and with certainty we know that God would never want us to be tormented (see 1 John 4:18). Torment also means under attack and besieged. Who but Satan himself would attack us and try to overtake us? And that's what fear does. It comes at us unawares and hits us when we're weak. Fear can overtake us if we let it. Remember the verse in 2 Timothy 1:7:

> **For God hath not given us the spirit of fear; but of power, and of love, and of a sound mind.**

This verse says we have a sound mind. This is the part that Satan, our greatest enemy, wants. He knows that if he can get us on a treadmill of fear, it will affect our minds. How does this happen? Rather than dwell on good thoughts that bring life, we focus on bad or negative thoughts that bring death and can bear no fruit. The fruits of the Holy Spirit, among others, are love, peace and joy (see Galatians 5:22-23). So when we are agitated, nervous, unusually tired and consequently, hard to get along with, we are most likely not of a sound mind — we are ruled by a spirit of fear and won't even know it. When our burden of fear is lifted through concerted prayer, then we once again experience love, peace and joy. Our minds will now have soundness and clarity, and we'll know where we're at and where we're going. But if we are living by a spirit of fear, confusion will abound, and there will be no soundness of mind.

    A sound mind is one that is filled with faith. It is a sure thing, not a doubtful thing. Many times through the years since I've been married and since I graduated from university with a degree in education, I have applied for various teaching jobs. I did so because we felt we needed the extra income, and also because I felt that God gave me the ability to teach young minds and to help students get through difficult growing-up years. All of my reasons for wanting to teach are good, and there is nothing evil about wanting a job teaching. Yet when I would be offered a job, either full time or even substitute teaching, I had no peace about it. I would think that I should take the job because it seemed the right thing to do, but my heart was not in it, and I had no joy at the prospect of teaching, although I knew I would enjoy working with the students. Then, when I would find out I didn't get a job I had applied for, I would feel a tremendous sense of relief, whereas I should have been disappointed. So what was going on?

Finding Enjoyment

Many years ago, I started drawing, then later took a course in watercolor painting. I found it particularly relaxing and very enjoyable. Several years later, I joined an art club, took workshops and started painting in acrylics. I was also interested in photography and even started a greeting card business, and sold many of my photos and prints. I discovered I had a great love of creating art. I would lose myself in the creation of a painting or on a photo shoot in a gorgeous wooded area, or anyplace where there was a lake and wildlife, or urban settings where there were older historic buildings. But I never once thought that it was anything more than an enjoyable hobby.

Then one day, I felt the Lord very clearly say to me that out of everything I do, I would be the most successful as an artist. In fact, He had impressed me with this many times. Yet, I couldn't seem to get it into my head that art could be a career or something I would ever take seriously. Knowing my thoughts, the Lord began to show me the importance of sharing my art with others and not hiding my talent under a bushel. He showed me how some of my paintings had the ability to lift people out of a depressed or tired state of mind and encourage them, bringing them peace with the thought of the image and what it could mean to them. For instance, if I took a picture of a pier on a quiet summer's eve, with blue water serenely flowing in the background, people would sense that peace and feel a moment of joy in an otherwise hectic day. So I began to believe that the thing that I loved to do the most is also what God wants me to do because it brings me such joy and brings peace to others. Since my days of creating photo cards, I expanded my card lines to include jewelry and unique watercolor images, which sell at local art galleries and gift shops.

This is not to say that teaching is out of the question. This is to say that God does not work by guilt and fear, but by joy and peace. I was a sales consultant for a prestigious kitchen-ware company. The products were sold by me going into people's homes, and cooking for them, and showing them the wonderful cooking utensils, cookware and bakeware, which they would then purchase for their own use. In order to maintain my status as a consultant and keep the points I had accumulated towards a raise and other rewards, I had to hold at least one cooking show every other month, and it had to reach a certain dollar amount.

At first, I wondered if I would be able to do this. I really loved the product and also selling it. There was never any question that the product would sell itself. I just wondered how long I would be able to hold shows. But God kept that door open, and after awhile, rather than fret that I couldn't meet my quota, I just left it in His hands and prayed that if He wanted me to continue, I would trust

Him to keep opening the doors. I really hoped that I would stay with the company because of the wonderful friends I had met, not to mention I was enjoying cooking for the first time ever. So God kept that door open. If I were not meant to continue, He would close that door, other things would take precedence over it, and I would no longer have joy or peace about selling the products.

Beware of the Enemy

How do we know when we are under a tormenting spirit of fear? We have no peace. We have trouble sleeping, and our thoughts are not clearly focused. We may feel guilt, pain, remorse and anger, plus any number of other negative emotions that we will think are ours to own and deal with. And here's the important point — once we realize that we are being plagued and tormented by these thoughts and realize the unwelcome source is Satan, then the doors will swing wide open, and we will be set free from fear by just a whisper of Jesus name. This has happened to me time and again, and I know to others as well. But we must discern the source of our pain and torment. This is where the Word of God comes in.

2. Become Proactive Against Fear

The second area is to become proactive against fear by arming ourselves with faith. The Bible says that we are not only children of God (see Romans 8:16-17), but we are also soldiers in God's army (see 2 Timothy 2:3-4). This is a strange dichotomy — both children and soldiers. How do the two mix? As children of God, we have every privilege of being His son or daughter as outlined in the Scriptures. We are heirs to the promises, both in this life and in the next life. The Bible is filled with the promises of God to His children. Some of our promises are just given, freely and as a result of Jesus' death on the cross for us. They have nothing to do with our works at all. Others are a direct result of our faithfulness and obedience to Him. Obviously, the more we obey, the more we benefit from His promises. As children, we are loved, protected and secure (see Psalm 91). We are to have the faith of a child and Jesus even said that unless we have the faith of a child, we cannot enter the kingdom of heaven (see Luke 18:17). This is when we are without fear and our minds are sound — we trust our loving heavenly Father to provide for all of our needs and love us enough to take care of us. There is nothing complicated about that kind of faith.

Be Prepared for Battle

As soldiers, we wear a different hat. No one really wants to be a soldier, but when you are caught in the middle of a battle, you will either fight back or be killed. Most of us fail to even realize we're in a battle, much less take up arms and fight back. But if we live in fear or are fearful and tormented in any way, then we know that we are a standing target, and we'd better do something. Sometimes it's obvious when we're under attack, like when a loved one snaps at us and says something unkind that hurts us. But most of the time, the attack is very subtle, so subtle that we don't even know we've been hit.

My father was a soldier during the Second World War and was called to the front lines near Rimini, Italy. His company was being attacked by heavy gunfire, and they started running to another area. He was running with heavy two-way radio equipment, and so it slowed him down

Chapter 8 - Exploring New Territory

enough that the enemy opened fire and shot him through the thighs. He said that at first he didn't even know he had been hit until a hot feeling went through his legs. He fell to the ground and lay there until another soldier turned back, noticed him, then ran back and picked him up, carrying him to their safe hide-out. Even though my father was trained, he couldn't run because he wasn't dressed properly by no fault of his own — he was carrying too much weight. Are we dressed properly for the battle we are engaged in?

We find our battledress outlined in detail in Ephesians 6:11-17:

> *Put on the whole armour of God, that ye may be able to stand against the wiles of the devil (11). For we wrestle not against flesh and blood, but against principalities, against powers, against the rulers of the darkness of this world, against spiritual wickedness in high places (12). Wherefore take unto you the whole armour of God, that ye may be able to withstand in the evil day, and having done all, to stand (13). Stand therefore, having your loins girt about with truth, and having on the breastplate of righteousness (14); And your feet shod with the preparation of the gospel of peace (15); Above all, taking the shield of faith, wherewith ye shall be able to quench all the fiery darts of the wicked (16). And take the helmet of salvation, and the sword of the Spirit, which is the word of God (17):*

In every verse, action is required, except when we see the word "stand" in verse 11. Does this mean we do nothing? It means, simply, that we stand, unafraid, for if we are dressed properly, none of his attacks and poisonous arrows will touch us. Imagine the Knights of old fully dressed in steel armour, every part of their body covered. This is how we must appear, a formidable foe to Satan, unmoveable and impenetrable. We must not give him any ground, but rather, make him afraid of us because we have the power in Jesus name to send him running. Faith builds confidence and enables us to show no fear because we know God is on our side (see Romans 8:31).

3. Explore New Thoughts & Ideas

Finally, and this is the third and last point, with fear gone and faith in operation, we can now proceed through new doors of thinking and explore new thoughts and ideas. Faith-filled thoughts widen our territory and open up many more possibilities for us. When we follow the Lord and trust in His many promises, there is no limit to what we can do. With expanded thinking, our lives take on much more meaning, and we can enjoy life as we're meant to. Sometimes all we have to do is ask God to expand our lives, and He will.

When I was working for Via Rail, and things were going well, I found that my interests in my spare time were limited. So I asked God to give me new interests. Soon, I found that I was interested in history, so I joined the Historical Society. Next, I found I was interested in geography and nature, so I joined a Naturalists Club and learned all about canoeing, rock climbing, and bird watching. A few years later, I found I liked photography, so now I could combine my interest in history and nature and take photos of them as well. Photography became an art form that led to other art forms, and eventually got me into computer design. I went from greeting cards to postcard design and even web design. Later, I got into sewing and made art quilts, bed quilts, and creative clothing designs.

The Lord continues to expand my interests and creativity in many different mediums, and it all started with a simple request. The Lord wants you to have an abundant life, too. This is one of His many promises and one we need to take hold of and live by (see John 10:10).

In the next chapter, we're going to look at how life can become a balancing act with so many responsibilities, and how we can learn to handle the many stressful situations we may face.

Footpath to Freedom

Chapter 9
Balancing Act

After I asked God to give me new interests, I realized a few years later that when you ask God for something, He answers you in big ways. He didn't just give me a couple of new interests, He gave me a whole bunch of them, and He continues to give me new ones. Being a generous and loving Heavenly Father, there is nothing He won't do for us or give us. My mother has been a shining example of a parent who gives and gives and gives. If we are in the store and I tell her I like something, she will either buy it right then (if she can) or I will find it in a Christmas gift bag or box on Christmas morning. She doesn't miss a thing, and I love her dearly for her thoughtfulness towards me. If I tell her I need clothes, she will go clothes shopping for me and buy me the most beautiful outfits that I need and wear a lot. If my mother does this, imagine what God does for us if we but ask?[1]

After awhile, I found that I had so many interests I couldn't get to them all. As mentioned, I was interested in history and nature, and then I turned towards photography and the arts. Plus, I took university courses in English and political studies, as well as many other subjects that greatly interested me, like sociology and psychology, and even some aspects of science. Each of these disciplines opened up many more avenues of thought and interests for me. Five years later, I returned to university and took two more years to complete my Bachelor of Education degree.

---
[1] My dear mother has since gone home to glory where she is with Jesus in His heaven.

Here, I developed new skills and interests in the field of education, mainly the psychology of learning, what makes children and youth tick, and also several creative ways to plan and teach a lesson. Through research, I further developed my writing skills, which began a career in book writing (rather than just freelance writing for newspapers and magazines, which I had done before) and book publishing.

The Importance of Prioritizing

So I had a new problem — what to do first? If you are anything like me, 24 hours in a day never seem to be enough time to do all the things I want to do. With so many interests and just day-to-day duties, life can very often become a balancing act, juggling schedules and trying to prioritize what needs to be done first. This can be fun at first, but after awhile it is easy to become over-involved and then get into a routine of always being on the run, going here, going there, volunteering our time and resources, which is all good, until life becomes too frenzied. God gave us only 24 hours in a day (take away at least 8 hours sleep) because He knew it would be all that our limited bodies (only made of dust) could really handle.

When we are always on the go, not only are we stressing our minds and bodies, but very often than not, it will also affect our relationships. We will miss that needed time with a spouse, child, or parent. We will not have time to call our friends, much less get together with them for a visit. And it can affect our health if we continue on a fast-paced schedule, not giving ourselves time to relax and recuperate in between. Also, if we are already overstressed and something comes up or happens on top of our already busy involvements, it could very well push us over the edge and may even affect us so adversely that everything piled up will make us come to a complete halt. Then we will be good for nothing and helpful to no one.

Beware of Over-extending Yourself

Also, sometimes major changes in our lives overextend us. If you think of the cycles of life, we are always active and involved, from the time we begin grade school to the time we graduate. After graduation, we are busy getting an education, and then we graduate and begin work. Some of us get married and are busy adjusting to married life, and then when children come along, life becomes even more complicated. Our work schedules may easily seem to extend to a 24-hour day until the children are grown. Meanwhile, our parents begin aging, and they need extra care.

I once heard a female Christian counselor and author talk about women who reach their mid-life, or menopause years. She said it is one of the most stressful times of her whole life, because her hormones are changing and depleting her of energy, her children are teenagers and may be a great cause for concern, and her parents are aging and need her extra help. She may find herself running to her parents' aid, caring for them and running them back and forth to the doctor, as well as catering to her children, who may also be old enough to be getting married. Now she has to help plan a wedding. Families may be financially stressed to the max at this time as well. All of these things combined spell anxiety and stress. A person in such a state might well wonder, Where is this abundant life promised when we're overly stressed and caught in the middle of a hurricane of activity?

We have all likely experienced bad stress, as in the above situations, when we become exhausted, anxious and worried, which drains us of everything. But there is also good stress. Good stress is when we're excited about things, and even though we are tired from a flurry of wonderful and enjoyable activity, we are not exhausted in a bad way. The excitement we feel and the anticipation of good things actually boost our energy levels. This is how I felt when I knew I'd be getting married. When my husband and I realized God was bringing us together for a lifetime commitment to marriage, we made a decision to get married immediately, as we didn't want to be apart any longer than necessary. We were about to engage in a very good, but stressful situation.

Life-Change Stress

We got engaged in the fall, and I had always wanted an outdoor wedding, so we set the date for as soon as possible before the weather turned colder and while there were still leaves on the trees that would be turning all the gorgeous fall colors. Because we had only about three weeks, give or take a couple of days, we had a lot to do in a very short time. I was so pleased that my very talented sister offered to plan the wedding and even put on a shower for me in that short time. Other family members helped too. Everyone had a part in making it the most beautiful wedding a bride could ever hope for.

I remember making lists every day during those frenzied three weeks. I was both excited and nervous, and had so much to think about that I slept very little, ate

Chapter 9 - Balancing Act

little, and lost lots of weight. I was also working full time at the time, but my mind was focused on my fiancé and the big-awaited day. After we were married, my husband and I were both exhausted since things had happened so quickly and so wonderfully. I was still working full time, but found it more difficult to continue in my job, so a couple of months later, we agreed that I should resign and continue to pursue my writing and artistic interests, which at the time, was running a small photography business. It took many months, but after awhile I was able to partially recuperate and get the rest I needed. My husband, however, did not get the same amount of time to rest.

After we first got married, Craig was very happy, but also shared he was feeling a little overwhelmed by all his new responsibilities. Almost overnight, he was given a wife to support, love and cherish, and her feline friend, Meesha to contend with. To add to his responsibilities, nine months later, we lived out of boxes for awhile and moved into a larger apartment, then moved again to a house we had bought in a resort town 45 minutes north of the city.

So now Craig had the additional burden of driving to and from work each day. Plus, there were many things he needed to do around the house and yard. He found he barely had time for me, let alone for himself, yet I marveled that he managed to balance everything in his life and still keep his sanity, and keep us together as a couple. Some people can handle stress much better than others.

Through the years, and especially recently, I have learned a lot from my husband. For one thing, he doesn't make someone else's problems his own. He will do whatever he can to help a person, but he knows when to say no and when its time to back off. Although he deeply cares about others, he doesn't get emotionally entangled with a person like I might, so he doesn't have the added stress of emotional and/or mental complications.

The Bane of Busyness

In my own situation, after about three years of glorious married life, I noticed that busyness was stealing away our time together. Busyness and stress, if we let them, can affect not only our relationships but can start to harden and even deaden our hearts. Rather than the fresh, anointed, and full heart of God-given love we start out with, our hearts become cold because we are too tired and haven't taken the time to communicate with each other.

Through our marriage, I could draw parallels between my life and my relationship with the Lord Jesus Christ. How easy it is to slack off and not spend precious time with the Lord each day in prayer and Bible reading. I remember feeling this same way — that my heart was changing after a few years of knowing the Lord. One day, it was as if I had lost the zeal of evangelism and the joy of the early days after being miraculously delivered from a life of slavery to sin. The cares of life and this world can so easily creep in, and we can become entrapped by busyness.

I could see it happen in my own life, but like a rushing tide of flood waters, it can overtake you if you're not prepared for it. When things start to escalate and you see what is starting to happen to your time and the state of your relationships, especially your own heart, that's the time to rein in your schedule and start dropping some involvements and commitments. You know it's time to turn to the Lord and elicit His help.

Chapter 9 - Balancing Act

In the Book of Revelation, Jesus pointed out to the church of Ephesus that they had lost their way, and He rebuked them for their lack of love for Him:

> *I know thy works, and thy labour, and thy patience, and how thou canst not bear them which are evil: and thou hast tried them which say they are apostles, and are not, and hast found them liars: And hast borne, and hast patience, and for my name's sake hast laboured, and hast not fainted. Nevertheless I have somewhat against thee, because thou hast left thy first love. Remember therefore from whence thou art fallen, and repent, and do the first works; or else I will come unto thee quickly, and will remove thy candlestick out of his place, except thou repent.*
> **Revelation 2:2-5**

Notice that they are a busy church, working tirelessly for the Lord, yet the Lord did not want them to neglect their time spent with Him. Why is love so important? Remember in the last chapter that "perfect love casts out fear." When we spend time with the Lord, we are also loving Him, and He will reveal His love to us. The more we know He loves us, the more we will trust Him and the less fear we will have.

Also, when we spend time with the Lord, we develop a closer relationship with Him. As we lean into Him, we get stronger because we are more dependent on Him than when we are just doing everything ourselves, blindly hoping it all works out. And we discover that He really is looking out for our welfare, and He doesn't want us leading stressful lives. He wants us to come to Him and lay our burdens down at His feet. The proof is in the following verses:

> *Be careful for nothing; but in every thing by prayer and supplication with thanksgiving let your requests be made known unto God. And the peace of God, which passeth all understanding, shall keep your hearts and minds through Christ Jesus. Philippians 4:6-7*
>
> *Casting all your care upon him; for he careth for you. 1 Peter 5:7*

Benefits of Fellowship

In addition to personal devotions, we need to fellowship with each other. When we do so, we can find help and support instead of struggling through things alone. This is what Scripture says about it:

> *Bear ye one another's burdens, and so fulfil the law of Christ. Galatians 6:2.*

Also, when we spend time together in meaningful fellowship, we start to open up to each other and learn about each other's needs. Bible studies are wonderful for this, as each member of the group becomes transparent and shares their deepest needs. Even in the natural or physical world, people have learned the great value in working with and for each other, otherwise called "networking." In the resort area where our house is, there is a networking group available for women who own businesses. They support each other's businesses and also pass each other's name onto valuable contacts through advertising and word of mouth. There are many networking groups all over the globe. In a world that can seem overwhelming, lonely, distant and cold, we are wise to look out for each other and try to help one another, so that no one is overburdened by the many cares of this life.

There is another very simple verse to remember that will help us live a balanced life:

> **But seek ye first the kingdom of God, and his righteousness; and all these things shall be added unto you. Matthew 6:33**

This is a no-fail promise of God and works for me every single time. It may be as simple as saying a prayer and reading a verse, as God directs. But it certainly has to do with our heart — we must seek Him first and not lose the passion and sincerity of loving and serving our first love — the Lord Jesus Christ.

Waiting on the Lord

Finally, when things seem too overwhelming, and we don't know which way to turn, we must take time to be quiet before the Lord. We have another sure promise when we do so:

> **But they that wait upon the LORD shall renew their strength; they shall mount up with wings as eagles; they shall run, and not be weary; and they shall walk, and not faint. Isaiah 40:31**

You may be reading this and feel so exhausted that you can hardly believe that reading a verse in the Bible will even begin to make a difference in your harried, frantic life. But the more time you take to read, the more you will start to believe, and your mind will change from carnal to spiritual as God reveals His Word and then fills you with His peace just for obeying Him.

In the final chapter, we're going to talk about the importance of our dreams and how we can use our particular giftings to open up new possibilities for us.

Chapter 10
Dare to Dream

Sometimes we can get so caught up and even comfortable in our regular routines that we forget to dream and give ourselves permission to dream. I remember when I was young, I lived in a world of make-believe dreams. I dreamed of one day being an evangelist and preaching to thousands of teenagers. I thought I'd live out of a Greyhound bus with my husband and travel all over North America. I had other dreams too, like living high up on a mountain, where my house was practically carved out of the rock of the mountain, and I'd enjoy a beautiful scenic drive to work each day in a nearby city I could see from my home. I believe that with some exceptions, almost everything that happens to us is as a result of a dream we once hoped for. And I believe that God inspires many of our dreams, so that His will is fulfilled through us.

Dreams can fill us with hope and can energize us to accomplish great tasks. They can also pull us out of a depressed or negative state of mind. I can remember that while growing up, I suffered from depression. One of the things that helped me was reading fictional books. These books are written in such a way that I could picture each scene and feel as if I were part of the story. Then, when I began my own writing, I discovered that I could create any scene I wanted and even give life to my characters. For many hours, I would be lost in writing my story, fascinated to see how it was unfolding.

Footpath to Freedom

The power of words can build a community, a civilization, a town, a city, a nation, a world, and a universe — the only limitation is our mind. I could research a place so well I would feel as if I'd been there myself, and then pass it on to my readers. I believe that most, if not all, fiction books are the visual result of someone's imagination, someone who loved to dream. But even in non-fiction, I've enjoyed describing real scenes that can change a person's mood and transport them to another place and time, like in the story below. The first full-length non-fiction book I ever completed was about how my husband and I met. It was filled with details and little stories over the course of 15 years, from the time we met until our honeymoon. This is an excerpt from one of the sections of the book, "Our Engagement."

The Day of Our Engagement

We chose Lake Louise, in mid-afternoon on Tuesday in mid-September, to get engaged. I regretted that I had worn my heavier sweatshirt instead of a light t-shirt, but the day before, trudging up Sulphur Mountain in Banff, the weather was deep fall, crisp, windy, and uncomfortably cold. It is amazing that I had even noticed the weather, since all of my thoughts were focused on my beloved Craig.

The path that meanders along Lake Louise to the tea house takes about one to two hours to walk. We couldn't wait to get there, so we did something unexpected. We climbed up the side of the mountain; Craig was behind me to make sure I didn't slip. People leisurely strolled by us, as if what we were doing was a normal occurrence.

I could see the lake shimmering through the mountainous trees. What a beautiful sight — the natural *wonders of God's majestic creation surrounding us. Lake Louise is a clear emerald green color, so clear you can see the sandy lake bottom. Surrounding it are magnificent towering mountains, some of them snow-covered. This day, there were little red canoes dotted in the distance. There were lots of people and tourists walking the paths, and outside the Chateau, a few tour buses were parked ... the mountains seemed to provide a symbolic knowing as they reached so high into the clouds, close to God, the Person we knew had put us together. It was as if they echoed far into the heavens the joy and celebration of our love, announcing it triumphantly to the Creator. It was that unexplainable knowing — I knew that God knew all along my deepest heart's desires. He knew I wanted to marry a man who loved God, like I did, and who would be willing to serve Him no matter what the cost.*

I looked around His creation ... the mountains — solid and immovable like the Promises of God. The water was glistening, clear and clean, bright green and silvery blue, like I imagine the streams in heaven. The carpets of tall, gorgeous fir trees were draped across the mountains, dressing the mountains like a groom's collar just before the ceremony. God was doing something marvellous, and I was both elated and unsure of myself, for I knew that He was entrusting me with the most intimate and spiritually binding relationship on earth — the bond of a husband and wife.

Word Pictures

Words, properly used, can change the way we think and can change a negative picture to a positive, peaceful one. Many Scriptures in the Bible are poetically written. Kind

David, as well as a king and a warrior, was also a psalmist, meaning he was a writer of songs or poems. One of the most poetic psalms he wrote is Psalm 23, also one of my favorites. Notice the visual description:

> *The LORD is my shepherd; I shall not want. He maketh me to lie down in green pastures: he leadeth me beside the still waters. He restoreth my soul: he leadeth me in the paths of righteousness for his name's sake. Yea, though I walk through the valley of the shadow of death, I will fear no evil: for thou art with me; thy rod and thy staff they comfort me. Thou preparest a table before me in the presence of mine enemies: thou anointest my head with oil; my cup runneth over. Surely goodness and mercy shall follow me all the days of my life: and I will dwell in the house of the LORD for ever.*

We must remember that most of David's writings were written when he was under great duress, either running away from enemies who wanted him killed or while hiding out before engaging in battle. He was not sitting comfortably in his palace, untouched by life's problems. When we read the Psalms, we find that David learned that when we dwell on the goodness of God, our hearts and minds will fill with peace, and gone will be the tormenting fears that try to assail us. Is it any wonder we are exhorted to meditate on the Scriptures to build our faith and give us peace of mind (see Romans 10:17)?

The Right Dreams

Also, we must be careful that our dreams do not lead us to the tents of wickedness. They must be God-approved and God-inspired. Many years ago, I was single and trying

Chapter 10 - Dare to Dream

to support myself working full-time and also working towards a degree in English through night school. I struggled financially many times, and especially when I had to take a year off from work due to emotional and physical health problems. A friend called, who had also been struggling with financial setbacks. It seemed that we were both dreaming big, and as writers and creative people, we knew no bounds for what we could do with the talents God had given us. But being single and having to support ourselves made it much more difficult to see these dreams fulfilled.

My friend, having spent valuable time with the Lord in prayer and reading the Scriptures, shared what the Lord had given her and felt she should pass it on to me. She gave me the following Scripture, which I never forgot:

> *For a day in thy courts is better than a thousand. I had rather be a doorkeeper in the house of my God, than to dwell in the tents of wickedness.*
> *Psalm 84:10*

When she shared the Scripture, we talked about being humble and that all the riches of the world, even the nicest house with all the most beautiful furniture, a new car or the ability to travel wordwide could never compare to the beauty of the Lord and to be in His presence. When we are in the presence of God, all our needs are fulfilled. I love the image of this verse. I can picture a golden mansion, where being a doorkeeper would seem the highest of honors, just to be in the presence of our God.

A Dream Come True

I mentioned earlier that I took up photography. Little did I know where this interest in photography would take me, both physically and in terms of my future! I would go for drives to the city park, where there are English gardens filled with every kind of fragrant and colorful flower and foliage imaginable. I'd take close-ups of wild roses, pale pink and pearly white, or I'd drive out of town and find the most extraordinary hide-outs. I found a historic tea house right along the river, walkways and gardens offering a spectacular view. Here I took photos of extraordinary cabbage flowers, in all different colors. I'd go through the city zoo and photograph every kind of animal. I'd drive out of town to nature parks and take photos of birds in flight, or birds landing. It seemed wherever I went, I started noticing nature's beauty all around me. I found myself enjoying my new hobby so much that I would often forget all about my troubles.

I stored the photos in albums and found myself looking at the photos often. If I were feeling down, I would start feeling better. When people came over, I'd be so excited to show them my pictures, and I noticed their enjoyment of them as well. One day, a friend came by, looked at all the pictures I had taken, liked them, and then suggested to me, "Why don't you make them into cards and sell them?" I had to think about that. Were they really good enough to offer others? So I prayed about it, and the answer that came to me was that to keep them closed up in the photo album would rob others of the chance to enjoy them, and perhaps they could be used to encourage others who also needed a lift. I had never thought of it that way, that I was not using it to bless others. The following Scripture immediately came to mind:

> *Let your light so shine before men, that they may see your good works, and glorify your Father which is in heaven. Matthew 5:16*

Later the Lord directed me to read the parable of the talents found in Matthew 25:14-30. If He gives us gifts, then He expects us to use them, whatever they might be. So I dared to start making photo cards and seeing if people were interested in buying them. They were, and soon I started selling them to retail stores, then found myself running it as a small business. Today, I still run the business, which has expanded to include my many artworks and now books.

I have read many encouraging stories of people who turned their talents into businesses or ministries that help countless people. People who love baking and cooking have used this gift to provide a good meal and hospitality to others who would otherwise be alone. While growing up, almost every Sunday, my mother prepared a great meal and would invite people over for food and fellowship. Everyone loved her delicious cinnamon buns, and whoever came for a visit would take home a dozen or so. What a tremendous gift to people who don't cook or don't have time or the expertise to bake!

Sharing Your Giftings

Dare to dream — there are hundreds and thousands of people out there with needs, and some of them can best be reached by your particular giftings. Often, when we begin to share our talents, they multiply, and the Lord blesses our labor. When I first began renting a table at Christmas craft shows, all I had to sell were my cards. Now I sell cards, books, jewelry, agates, my sewing creations, and published books. But the greatest benefit in selling our wares is that we meet new people and also pick up new ideas. We make new friends, even if only for a season. No matter what your particular giftings are there is always room to grow. And there are so many opportunities to learn new things. But regardless of what we do, whether we create things or go to a regular job each day, we must always remember that God wants to use us wherever we are. He gives us dreams not only for our pleasure and enjoyment, but also for the sake of the people we will meet along the way. It is a good thing to have dreams — you never know where they will take you and how much good you can do with your talents. God wants us to move forward and move on — this is difficult to do without a vision, a dream, and a goal.

Sometimes we may find ourselves in a rut. We do the same things day in and day out. We eat the same meals, wear the same clothes and go to the same restaurants. Our minds become dull and we lose the excitement of life. We think that traveling, or perhaps moving to another location, will jar us out of this lull, but most often we can make changes right where we are if only we would reach out and try something different.

A Fresh Vision

Clearly, God wants us to have a fresh vision. We don't have to settle for a mundane life because nothing seems to be changing. It is up to us to pursue our future and, prayerfully, move forward, believing that God will work all things out for the good. When it comes to having a vision of our present and future, God is all for it. This was revealed to my husband one day when he was reading the Bible, and a verse jumped out at Him:

> ***Where there is no vision, the people perish: Proverbs 29:18***

This was hugely significant to him, and he explained that this is what was happening to some churches that are not progressively moving forward, but find themselves in a rut. They have lost their vision and are not hot to bring about the Kingdom of God in a world that is thirsting for truth. I have heard astonishing testimonies of people with a heart for ministry who started out with nothing but a prayer and then saw God miraculously provide what they needed. Embracing a vision and prayerfully and boldly releasing it into the world is extremely important and far-reaching. Remember, faith is substance and evidence (see Hebrews 11:1). God gives us a vision when we believe. We must first believe, and then we will see.

The beginning of this book talks about freedom and the way out of the many prisons we may find ourselves in, especially the ones caused by sin and fear. We start with Jesus, and we continue with Jesus. He has made it possible for us to live a life of complete freedom if we just follow His Manual and read His instructions, which will always work for us no matter what. In reading this, I hope you have discovered the footpath to freedom, and that you will continue to walk in that freedom. Please take time to share your insights and experiences with others in need of freedom as well.

I leave you with the following Scripture and encourage you to continue exploring God's incredible Book, the Bible, and talk with Him often. He waits for you, He listens, and He will teach you more, much more, about the way to walk in His freedom.

> *Stand fast therefore in the liberty wherewith Christ hath made us free, and be not entangled again with the yoke of bondage. Galatians 5:1*

The Way of Salvation

In all of life, no one loves you more than God does. He loved you so much He sent His own Son to die on a cross, then He raised Him up again, and He lives forever more. When Jesus died, a phenomenal thing happened -- He willingly took all our sins and sicknesses upon Himself, so that we wouldn't have to bear them ourselves. He forgave us the huge debt of sin we owed to God, so that we could be pardoned, and set free to live a life unto Him. Salvation is free, and open to all who call upon the name of the only One who can truly save us. If you haven't already taken this important step, you are invited to accept Jesus into your heart and life today. Begin by reading the following Scriptures to begin your new life, and don't delay!

Today is the day of salvation ...

(For he saith, I have heard thee in a time accepted, and in the day of salvation have I succoured thee: behold, now is the accepted time; behold, now is the day of salvation.) 2 Corinthians 6:2

We are all in need of salvation ...

For all have sinned, and come short of the glory of God; Romans 3:23

Good works cannot save you ...

They are all gone out of the way, they are together become unprofitable; there is none that doeth good, no, not one. Romans 3:12

Not by works of righteousness which we have done, but according to his mercy he saved us, by the washing of regeneration, and renewing of the Holy Ghost; Titus 3:5

The Lord will never turn away anyone who truly wants to know Him ...

For whosoever shall call upon the name of the Lord shall be saved. Romans 10:13

Jesus is the only One who can save us ...

Neither is there salvation in any other: for there is none other name under heaven given among men, whereby we must be saved. Acts 4:12

That at the name of Jesus every knee should bow, of things in heaven, and things in earth, and things under the earth; Philippians 2:10

Salvation gives us eternal life with Jesus ...

For God so loved the world, that he gave his only begotten Son, that whosoever believeth in him should not perish, but have everlasting life. John 3:16

For God sent not his Son into the world to condemn the world; but that the world through him might be saved. John 3:17

But every person is condemned without Jesus ...

He that believeth on him is not condemned: but he that believeth not is condemned already, because he hath not believed in the name of the only begotten Son of God. John 3:18

The Way Of Salvation

We have an assurance of salvation ...

And I give unto them eternal life; and they shall never perish, neither shall any man pluck them out of my hand. John 10:28

My Father, which gave them me, is greater than all; and no man is able to pluck them out of my Father's hand. John 10:29

Dear Friend,

If you would like to receive Jesus into your heart and life today and also have the assurance that you will spend eternity in heaven with Him, please begin by saying this prayer:

Dear Heavenly Father,

I come to you in the name of Jesus. Your Word says, "Whosoever shall call upon the name of the Lord shall be saved" (Acts 2:21). I call on you now, and ask Jesus to come into my heart, forgive me for all my sins, and cleanse me. I ask you to be Lord over my life, according to Romans 10:9-10 — "That if thou shalt confess with thy mouth the Lord Jesus, and shalt believe in thine heart that God hath raised him from the dead, thou shalt be saved. For with the heart man believeth unto righteousness; and with the mouth confession is made unto salvation." I do this now — I confess that Jesus is Lord, and I believe in my heart that God raised Him from the dead.

In Jesus Name,
Amen

You are now reborn! You are a Christian and a child of God! Be assured, you have taken the most important step of your life, and God has reserved your place in heaven. He will always be with you, and lead you into all truth:

> **But the Comforter, which is the Holy Ghost, whom the Father will send in my name, he shall teach you all things, and bring all things to your remembrance, whatsoever I have said unto you. John 14:26**

> **...for he hath said, I will never leave thee, nor forsake thee. Hebrews 13:5b**

You will need to read the Bible on a daily basis to get to know Him, and all the many promises He has for you. As well, don't delay in contacting a Bible-believing church, where you will find fellowship with others who have also taken this important life-changing step. May God bless you as you continue on your new path of life, and freedom in Christ!

About the Author

Linda McBurney-Gunhouse calls Manitoba, Canada, home, where she embraces both the quiet and challenges of life with a passion for writing. Her goal is to inspire others by sharing her journey of overcoming adversity and achieving personal growth. Alongside her non-fiction work, Linda has a deep love for storytelling, particularly in fiction.

With years of dedication to her craft, Linda has honed her writing skills through formal education and real-world experience. She holds a BA and B.Ed. in English, and has studied Journalism, English, and History. Additionally, she earned a diploma in magazine writing. Her career has seen her as a contributing editor for a community college newspaper, as well as an editor for a local newspaper in Winnipeg. She has also written extensively for several community newspapers, with her work also appearing in national, city, and regional outlets, books, and a specialized magazine. She dabbled in script writing for radio.

As an accomplished eBook author, Linda has written several inspirational books, including five full-length novels. Her works have garnered a global readership, with some titles frequently ranking in the Top 100 within their categories. She also blogs regularly, offering insightful, thought-provoking content.

Linda is passionate about sharing her faith and the lessons she's learned from overcoming life's obstacles in ways that resonate with her readers. She enjoys teaching Creative Writing and occasionally offers motivational speaking. She continues to contribute freelance writing to local newspapers and has facilitated both in-person and online writers' groups. When she's not writing, Linda enjoys exploring various forms of art and creativity.

Other Titles
By Linda McBurney-Gunhouse

Inspirational Books

Cures for Stress
Essential Steps to Increase Your Faith
Footpath to Freedom
Freedom Through Spiritual Discernment
Healing & Hope for Child Loss
Healing For The Wounded Soul
Loneliness: The Pathway to Discovery
Making Sense of the Rapture
Money: Master or Servant?
No Fear of Hell
Power Thoughts for Positive Thinking
Spiritual Leadership in a Fallen World
The Act of Decision-Making
The Bible: Conformed or Transformed?
The Journey of Oneness
The Journey to Contentment
The Power of Submission
Victory Over Backsliding
When Love Is All There Is

Biography

The Bonk Saga: A History of Memories
Called to Overcome

Devotionals

Pathways to Devotion I
Pathways to Devotion II
Pathways to Devotion III
Pathways to Devotion IV
Pathways to Devotion V
Pathways to Devotion VI
Pathways to Devotion VII
Pathways to Devotion VIII
Pathways to Devotion IX
Pathways to Devotion X
Pathways to Devotion XI
Pathways to Devotion XII

Fiction

The Redemption of Steep Rock Cove
Return to Steep Rock Cove
Christmas Comes to Steep Rock Cove
Waves of Change at Steep Rock Cove
Driving with the Top Down
Track Three
Joanna's Secret Treasure

Poetry Books

Heart Songs
Songs in the Desert
Water Crossings
Wings I: Morning Arising
Wings II: Daylight Reflections
Wings III: Contemplation
Wings: Inspirational Poetry Series

Creative How-to Books

Artistic Ideas & Inspirations
How to Create Stories From Your Own Life
Living a Creative Life

Writing Manuals

Creative Writing
Write Your Life Story
Fiction Writing

Please visit our website at www.creativefocus.ca to discover the many books from this list that are available as eBooks.

Note: If you have enjoyed reading this book, or any other eBook of mine, please rate it online, or recommend it on your Facebook page. It will help spread the word, and let others know it is available. My goal is to help, encourage and inspire others through my writing. Thank you and may God richly bless you!

www.ingramcontent.com/pod-product-compliance
Lightning Source LLC
LaVergne TN
LVHW012027060526
838201LV00061B/4501